THE ROMANS

THE ROMANS

An introduction

Antony Kamm

London and New York

First published 1995
by Routledge
11 New Fetter Lane, London EC4P 4EE

Simultaneously published in the USA and Canada
by Routledge
29 West 35th Street, New York, NY 10001

Typeset in Baskerville by
J&L Composition Ltd, Filey, North Yorkshire
Printed and bound in Great Britain by
Biddles Ltd, Guildford and King's Lynn

British Library Cataloguing in Publication Data
A catalogue record for this book is available from the British Library

Library of Congress Cataloguing in Publication Data
A catalogue record for this book has been requested

ISBN 0–415–12039–X
0–415–12040–3 (pbk)

For Eileen

CONTENTS

FIGURES

MAPS AND TABLES

ACKNOWLEDGEMENTS

I am grateful to Derry Jeffares, who encouraged me to write the original version of this book, and was the first to read it. The present text owes a great deal to the perceptive comments and constructive suggestions of Ronald Mellor, James Neville, and Boris Rankov. I have been fortunate, too, to have had such an experienced and sympathetic editor as Richard Stoneman, and to have been able to rely on the cheerful and efficient support of his editorial assistant, Vicky Peters. In Nigel Hope, Routledge supplied the ideal copy-editor: skilful, understanding, knowledgeable, and supremely diplomatic. I am indebted also to my colleagues Robin Sowerby, for help with sources, and Andrew Wheatcroft, for professional advice and assistance. The task of finalizing the text on disk and printing it out by means of an expiring word-processing system would hardly have been possible without the friendly expertise of Jim Shanks and Robert Sneddon.

In researching and obtaining illustrations I have received particular help from Michael Dixon, Helmut Jung (Deutsches Archaeologisches Institut, Rome), Brendan Moore and Bernard Jackson (British Museum), and D. J. Bateson (Hunterian Museum). All the coins (photographed by Glasgow University Photographic Services Unit) are from the Hunterian coin collection, founded in about 1770 by William Hunter himself.

A. K.
Dollar
Clackmannanshire

ALPS

ALPS

ALPS

ALPS

ALPS

Como
Milan
Cremona
Brixellum
R. Trebia
LIGURIA
CISALPINE GAUL
A P E N N I N E S
VENETIA
Verona
Padua
Mantua
R. Po
Aquileia
ISTRIA
Ariminum
Sarsina
R. Rubicon
R. Arno
UMBRIA
ETRURIA
Lake Trasimene
Assisi
R. Tiber
PICENUM
CORSICA
Cosa
Mt Ciminius
Reate
Fidenae
Tibur
Rome
Tusculum
Sulmo
Ostia
Alba Longa
Aricia
Arpinum
Laurentum
Lanuvium
SAMNIUM
Lavinium
Antium
Aquinum
LATIUM
Cannae
Tarracina
Capua
Caudine Forks
Venusia
Cumae
Nola
APULIA
Misenum
CAMPANIA
Puteoli
Pompeii
Brundisium
SARDINIA
Naples
Herculaneum
Tarentum
Capri
CALABRIA
LUCANIA
Rudiae
Heraclea
BRUTTIUM
Messana
SICILY
Syracuse

ITALY
(showing the places mentioned in the book)

1

THE FOUNDING OF ROME

Whoever coined the epigram 'Rome was not built in a day' –
and it was probably the sixteenth-century English dramatist John
Heywood – established a permanent reminder that the Roman
civilization was twelve hundred years developing, flourishing,
and ultimately disintegrating. This is a considerable time in
the history of thinking man: almost as long as from the Dark
Ages in Britain and the establishment of Islam in Arabia to the
present day, and over three times longer than the period since
the foundation of the first English settlement in Jamestown,
Virginia. It was, too, a thoroughly impressive epoch, which
had, and still commands, a profound influence on western
society.

The civilization of Rome owed most to ancient Greece, whose
golden age is generally regarded as having lasted from about 490
BC to the death in 323 BC of Alexander the Great. The Romans
were not great innovators. They learned what they could from
others and then applied that knowledge to their own needs and
purposes. They were dedicated and often ruthless in their pursuit of order and organization, and in the administration of their
own brand of firm, but inherently benevolent, imperialism. The
free-born Roman was not even a particularly hard worker. He
did not need to be: there was an accepted convention in the
ancient world that it was a mark of humanity to inflict slavery,
rather than slaughter or maiming, as a penalty for those on the
losing side in battle. This was the darkest aspect of imperialism.
The first-century BC scholar and philosopher Varro refers to
slaves as a 'species of articulate farming stock', as opposed to
'inarticulate stock' (oxen) and 'dumb stock' (carts), in his agricultural treatise (I. 17). In the first century AD, it is probable that

1

one in three of the population of Rome was a slave; this was also the proportion of negro slaves to whites in the American South in the 1850s.

The Roman era can be divided into three parts. The years from the founding of the city of Rome until 510 BC, when the last of its kings was ejected, are known as the period of the kings. The republic of Rome lasted from 509 until 27 BC, when Augustus established legal precedents for absolute rule. This was the beginning of the age of imperial Rome, that is rule by emperors. In AD 476, the sitting emperor in Rome, Romulus Augustulus, was deposed by Odoacer, a German, who ruled Italy as king. That action brought to an end the Roman empire in the west. An eastern empire carried on into the Middle Ages, until it finally collapsed in 1453, when Constantinople was captured by the Turk, Muhammad II.

The Romans themselves were in no doubt when Rome was founded: 21 April 753 BC. On that day of the year, too, they celebrated the traditional festival of the Parilia in honour of Pales, the god (or goddess – the Romans were notoriously vague about the gender of some of their deities) of shepherds and sheep. In 1948 traces were found on the Palatine Hill, the central and most easily fortified of the seven hills of the ultimate city, of the huts of a settlement of shepherd folk dating from about 750 BC. Current excavations have uncovered the remains of a ritual boundary wall of about the same period.

THE FOUNDING LEGENDS: ROMULUS AND AENEAS

The legend of the founding of Rome by Romulus was circulating 400 years later at the most. It tells how a local king, Numitor of Alba Longa, was ejected by his younger brother, Amulius. To secure his position, Amulius then murdered Numitor's sons and forced Numitor's daughter, Rhea Silvia, to become a vestal virgin, thus, he thought, preventing her from having any children, at least for the time being. Vestal virgins normally served as priestesses in the temple of Vesta for thirty years from between 6 and 10 years old, and the penalty for failing to remain virginal was a singularly nasty death. Rhea Silvia, however, caught the lascivious eye of the god Mars, who had his way with her while

2

she slept. The outcome of this unconscious but divine experience was twin sons, who were named Romulus and Remus.

There was a fine rumpus. Amulius had Rhea Silvia thrown into the river Tiber, where she sank conveniently into the arms of the god of the river, who married her. The twins were also consigned to the Tiber, but in a reed basket, which floated away until it was caught in the branches of a fig tree. They were suckled by a she-wolf (appropriately, for wolves were sacred to Mars) until the royal shepherd found them and rescued them. In another version of the story they were breast-fed by his wife, a former prostitute, who had just lost a stillborn child – the Latin word *lupa* means both 'she-wolf' and 'prostitute'.

The couple cared for Romulus and Remus and in due course revealed to them the circumstances of their birth. Amulius was killed in battle and their grandfather Numitor was restored to his throne. As a contribution to the ensuing celebrations, the

Figure 1   The bronze Capitoline wolf and twins is one of the most famous symbols of early Rome, though the wolf (85 cm high and dating from the end of the sixth or early fifth century BC), is Etruscan work. The twins were added in the fifteenth century AD. It is possible, however, that they were replacements. Cicero, in one of his Catiline speeches, refers to a statue of a wolf and twins on the Capitoline Hill that was struck by lightning in 65 BC, and it may well have been this wolf. (*Deutsches Archaeologisches Institut, Rome*)

brothers resolved to establish a new city near the spot where they had been washed ashore. They took omens by watching the flight of birds, which indicated that the city should be built on the Palatine Hill, on which Romulus was standing, and that he should be its king. Romulus then set about marking the boundary with a plough drawn by a white cow and a white bull. Remus, either in fun or as a gesture of derision, committed the impropriety of jumping over the furrow. Romulus lost his temper and killed his twin.

The embryo city, still no more than a settlement, was rather short of women. Romulus invited the neighbouring Sabine tribe to a programme of games he was organizing to mark the harvest festival. When the guests were comfortably settled, the Romans, as they were now known, abducted at swordpoint 600 Sabine daughters, all but one of them, it is said, virgins. In an addition to the traditional story, they proved to be sterile until Juno, goddess, among other things, of childbirth, took a hand and sorted out the problem. Or it may be that the Sabine women, having suffered abduction, refused at first to co-operate with their self-styled husbands.

A further tradition, well known at least by 240 BC, traces the origins of Rome to the even earlier time of the legendary Trojan hero, Aeneas, son of a mortal father and of the goddess Venus. He fought against the Greeks in the Trojan War, escaped from the sack of the city, and, after many wanderings, vicissitudes, and divine interventions, landed in Italy and founded the dynasty from which Romulus eventually came. This was the version of the story much favoured by the emperors of Rome, who liked to think of themselves as being nominally descended from the ancient heroes, and by the Romans themselves, who could thus see the early history of their city, which was one of continual struggle for survival, reflected in heroic legend. It was written up in verse by Virgil (70–19 BC), largely in response to the encouragement of Augustus, in the *Aeneid*, which was published posthumously. It is the national epic of the Roman empire, and the most famous poem of the Roman era.

According to the legend, and to Virgil, Aeneas cast anchor at the mouth of the Tiber.

Now, Aeneas, looking out from the glassy ocean, sees a vast stretch of forest. The river Tiber's pleasant stream flows

4

through it before bursting into the sea in swirling eddies made yellow by the copious sandy sediment. Above and all around, different kinds of birds indigenous to the river banks and reaches sweeten the air with song as they dart among the trees. Having ordered his companions to change course and steer for land, Aeneas is elated as he makes the river's shade.

(Aeneid, VII. 29–36)

The Tiber flowed through Latium, whose king, Latinus, had had divine intimation that he should hand over his daughter in marriage to a stranger. So he offers her to Aeneas, much to the discomfort of another local king, Turnus of the Rutuli, who fancies her for himself. Reluctantly drawn into war, Aeneas obtains the support of Tarchon, king of the Etruscans, and finally triumphs.

The historical sack of Troy was in about 1220 BC. To cover the period between the presumed arrival of Aeneas and the traditional date for the founding of Rome, the Romans invented a string of monarchs from Ascanius, son of Aeneas by his first (Trojan) wife, to Numitor. Though there is no firm tradition about Aeneas's death, there is an intriguing reference to a tomb in the Greek historian, Dionysius of Halicarnassus, who lived in Rome at the very end of the first century BC.

The Latins built a hero-shrine to Aeneas, inscribing it to him as 'The god and father of this place, who guides the waters of the Numicius [a river in Latium]'. . . . It is an earth mound, not very big, with trees set around it in regular rows – well worth seeing.

(Roman Antiquities, I. 64)

The shrine that Dionysius visited at Lavinium is almost certainly the seventh-century BC tumulus excavated in 1968. Originally it contained a burial chest, which was rifled about a hundred years later. The tomb was restored at the end of the fourth century BC.

So much for the legend. Historically, Latium and Etruria (land of the Etruscans) were crucial in the development of Rome into an autonomous and then an independent city state, though it is not known for certain where the original Latins and Etruscans came from. The Latins who first settled on the Palatine Hill, however, had been in the region since about 1000 BC. They herded sheep, goats, and cattle, and kept pigs. In the manner

5

of such people, they lived in small scattered communities, in round or oblong huts made of wooden poles interwoven with twigs and branches and then covered with clay.

THE SITE OF ROME

The summit of the hill itself was roughly trapezoidal in shape, the longest side being about 400 metres long. On three sides, the rock sloped steeply down into valleys which were often full of flood water. On the other, north-eastern, side, a narrow saddle of rock led to the adjoining hill. The cluster of hills, each between 60 and 100 metres high, stood on a plateau above the surrounding plain, the soil of which was continually enriched by deposits of volcanic silt from the Tiber and its tributaries. We may imagine, then, the summit of the Palatine Hill covered with clusters of small thatched huts of wood and clay, and somewhere a flat, open meeting space, the forerunner of the Roman forum. The burial place was in the marshy ground at the foot of the hill, where years later would stand the great forum of republican and imperial Rome. Only infants, and sometimes young children, appear to have been buried within the community.

The site was an inspired one for other reasons, too. The sea, with its potential for foreign trade, was only a few kilometres downstream. The hill overlooked the shallows which constituted the most convenient point for crossing the river as it neared the sea, and thus commanded the main route along western Italy. The city lay mid-way between the north and south of Italy, that natural formation of land enclosed by the Alps to the north, and by the sea everywhere else. Furthermore, Italy itself lay centrally in the Mediterranean, with ready access to the rest of Europe, to Africa, and to the east. Thus the fourteenth-century proverb, 'All roads lead to Rome', was true from the start. At much the same time as the first settlement on the Palatine Hill, the Greeks were taking advantage of the diffusion of the existing tribes in southern Italy, and were establishing sea-ports round the south and west coasts, and in Sicily. The port farthest north, and one of the first to be built, was Cumae on the Bay of Naples, within comparatively easy reach of Rome. Through these ports Rome had access to the Greek world; from the Greeks at Cumae, the Latins learned the Greek alphabet, which they adapted for their own use and language.

6

ETRUSCAN INFLUENCE

Etruria was immediately across the Tiber to the north. It was, unusually for the times, predominantly an urban society; its wealth came from trade and its supremacy through sea-power. The Etruscans were given to extravagant but extraordinarily varied decoration and artistic display, and to the worship of gloomy gods, from which the Romans derived some of the more repulsive features of their religious observances and public entertainment. In much the same way as their culture, the Etruscans' political philosophy took its origins from the east and its direction from the Greeks, while developing on lines distinctive to Italy.

At some time between 650 and 600 BC, the Etruscans crossed the Tiber in force and occupied Latium. It would have been now that the villagers on the Palatine Hill joined up with settlers on the other hills to form one united community, either in an attempt to fend off the Etruscan invaders, or to be brought in line with the Etruscan policy of imperial government by means of autonomous city states. From this point until the establish-ment of the republic in Rome (assuming Romulus to have been as mythical as his origins lead us to suppose), we have the names of six kings: Numa Pompilius, Tullus Hostilius, Ancus Marcius, Tarquinius Priscus (Tarquin the Elder), Servius Tullius, and Tarquinius Superbus (Tarquin the Proud). Though there is little doubt that all six existed – and the rule of six kings is enough to fill the time-gap between the historical founding of Rome and the republic – the main events of the period are so entwined with folklore that it is difficult to assign many of them accurately to a particular reign.

UNDER THE KINGS

The Roman talent for empire building first emerged in the period of the kings, even though the original intention may have been to survive by aggression and by dominating the local scene. Territory gained provided additional fighting power, and the kings of Rome succeeded in subjugating a fair slice of land south of the Tiber. The most significant advance to a position of supremacy among Latin states came with the defeat of Alba Longa. Destruction would be a better term, for nothing has

7

been found of that city of a date later than the sixth century BC. With that victory, the Romans assumed precedence in religious affairs in Latium, for they then took over the administration of the sacred festivals which had for years been celebrated on the Alban Mount. Servius Tullius transferred the regional festival of Diana from Aricia to the Aventine Hill of Rome, where he built a shrine to her. Shortly afterwards a massive temple, about 60 metres long and 50 metres wide, was dedicated on the Capitoline Hill to Jupiter, chief of the gods.

In this period, too, the roots of the later Roman constitution are to be found. The king was nominally appointed by the senate, an advisory body of patricians, members of a closed group of families of noble origins. He wielded much the same power over his subjects as that of a Roman head of family over his household, which included the right to inflict capital punishment. The king was also responsible for foreign relations and for war, for security, public works, justice, and the maintenance of religion. Wherever he went in public, he was accompanied by a band of attendants, or lictors, each carrying the *fasces*, a bundle of rods with an axe in the middle, signifying the punishments that could be meted out to criminals.

The concept of the father (Latin *pater*) was extended into the community at large. Each patrician family had its clients (from the Latin word meaning 'listener'), an extended body of hereditary hangers-on, who depended on the patricians for patronage and for economic support. In return for these favours they gave their labour and, in time of war, military service, in the same way as the villeins in medieval times. There was a sharp distinction between the patricians and their clients on the one hand, and the *plebs*, the common people, on the other. The community was divided, probably territorially, into three tribes, each responsible for providing 1,000 infantry and 100 cavalry in time of war, which came round frequently. Each tribe was further divided into ten *curiae*, whose representatives were responsible for civil affairs, and met together as required by the king to discuss, but not to decide upon, matters of national importance. Servius Tullius is credited with reforming the army, to which he also gave the status of a political assembly, the *comitia centuriata*.

We are a far cry from the notion of a primitive people scratching the soil and herding rudimentary flocks. Not only were craftsmen plying their various trades from the start, but under the first historical king of Rome, Numa Pompilius, they were properly represented by guilds, according to the first-century AD Greek historian and biographer, Plutarch. 'Numa divided the craftsmen according to their trades – flute-players, goldsmiths, carpenters, dyers, shoemakers, leather-dressers, potters, and workers in copper and brass. He created a further guild of all the other trades grouped together' (*Lives: Numa*, XVII). This diversity of crafts served a society which, unlike the Greeks, did not use money. Trade was conducted by barter (wood or wool for bronze, salt for pottery, corn for shoes, and so on) or, in cases where the system was inadequate, by expressing value in terms of head of cattle. A head of cattle (*pecus*) was the first Roman monetary unit, from which came the Latin word for money (*pecunia*); one head of cattle was equal to ten sheep. Latterly during the period of the kings, a primitive monetary system evolved based on ingots of raw copper, weighed on a clumsy balance which probably measured only a single standard unit, the Roman pound (*libra*) of 327 g. An ingot could then be broken up into lumps of different sizes and values. According to the historian and scientist Pliny the Elder (AD 23–79), 'King Servius first put a stamp on the copper; up until then, Timaeus [*c.* 346–*c.* 250 BC] says, they used raw metal. The stamped design was that of an ox or a sheep' (*Natural History*, XXXIII. 13).

The Etruscans had considerable skill in three aspects of building and civil engineering at which the Romans were to excel: road construction, hydraulics, and the use of the arch to bridge space – examples of Etruscan arches still survive at Volterra and Perugia. The planning of the great temple to Jupiter is attributed to Tarquinius Priscus, but his grandson Tarquinius Superbus supervised its building, calling up labour from Etruria as well as from Latium to get the job done. His zeal appears to have matched his pride.

> Having selected from the *plebs* those who were loyal to him and fit for military service, he put the rest to forced labour on public works. For he believed that kings were most vulnerable when the poor and needy were idle. He was also keen to complete during his reign the projects left unfinished by his grandfather. These included extending the drainage system, on which digging had begun, and adding a colonnade all round the amphitheatre race-track,

of which only the foundations had been built. The poor were set to work in return for a miserable ration of grain: quarrying stone, cutting timber, leading the wagons filled with these materials, or even themselves carrying the materials on their backs. Others were put to digging underground conduits, constructing arches and supporting walls for them, and assisting the various craftsmen, copper-smiths, carpenters, and stonemasons, all forcibly removed from their private businesses to labour for the public good.

(Dionysius of Halicarnassus, *Roman Antiquities*, IV. 44)

Pliny describes the dimensions of some of the underground sewers constructed at this time as 'large enough for a loaded hay-wagon to pass through' (*Natural History*, XXXVI. 24). The Cloaca Maxima (Great Sewer) of republican and imperial Rome was originally an open ditch, designed to drain the water from the valleys between the hills of Rome, including the ancient forum, and to collect the streams of other drains before discharging itself into the Tiber, where its arched exit can still be seen under the Ponte Palatino.

The Etruscans were also past masters at the art of delicate sculpture in terracotta. Tarquinius commissioned some Etruscan sculptors from Veii to fashion a chariot to stand on top of the new temple. According to Plutarch, when it was put into the furnace the clay, instead of contracting as the moisture evaporated, swelled up to such a size that the furnace had to be completely dismantled before the finished piece could be removed.

By the time the temple was completed, however, the period of the kings was over for good. The rape of the blameless Lucretia by the son of Tarquinius has proved a popular subject for art, literature, and even the stage ever since, but, if it ever took place, there is no evidence that it was the cause of the fall of Tarquinius. It is more likely that the rebellion by a band of nobles led by Lucius Junius (afterwards known as Brutus) was the natural reaction of a society which, on the Greek model, was verging towards democratic government, against a monarch who had exceeded his constitutional brief and made himself even more unpopular by his imposition of forced labour. It is possible, too, that the conspiracy was part of a wider revolt by several Latin

Figure 2   An example of Etruscan art in terracotta: a sarcophagus of 150–130 BC, surmounted by a life-size painted figure of Seianti Hanunia Tlesnasa. Inside it were found the bones and skull of a woman who was over 80 years old when she died. (*British Museum*)

cities, including Antium, Aricia, and Tusculum, against a king of Etruscan origin.

Rome was not yet entirely free. Tarquinius escaped and naturally commanded the support of the Etruscans, one of whose chiefs, known as Porsena, occupied Rome for some time by force. To this campaign belong the traditional stories of Horatius, who held the bridge against the advancing Etruscans, and of Mucius Scaevola, who plunged his right hand into the flames rather than reveal details of a plot to kill Porsena. Porsena, having previously survived one assassination attempt, was so unnerved by the thought of further ones, that he withdrew his garrison from the city in return for hostages.

Now the women too were inspired to emulate Scaevola's example. When the Etruscans, purely by chance, camped close to the banks of the Tiber, the girl Cloelia, one of the hostages, tricked the guards and swam the river under a hail of missiles and javelins at the head of a group of other girls, all of whom she restored safely to their dear ones in Rome.

11

When this was reported to Porsena, his first reaction was one of fury. He sent a deputation to Rome demanding that Cloelia be handed over; he said he didn't care about the others. Then, in admiration of a feat which he reckoned was more impressive even than Scaevola's, he announced that he would regard the treaty as having been broken if she were not handed over; if she were surrendered, however, he would send her back safe and sound.

Both sides behaved honourably. The Romans returned their surety of peace according to the terms of the treaty: Porsena gave her not only his personal protection but also further recognition. He offered to send back with her a certain number of hostages of her choice. The story goes that when they were all paraded, she picked out only young boys, as being more appropriate to her maidenly modesty. In the opinion of the other hostages this was sensible also in that it removed from the hostile environment those least able to look out for themselves.

(Livy, *History of Rome*, II. 13)

Etruscan attempts to recapture Rome, as well as Antium, Aricia, and Tusculum, smouldered on until 505 BC, when they were finally extinguished before Aricia: not by a Roman army but by a force of Greek auxiliaries from Cumae, called up to bolster the Latin army.

In the meantime, Rome had become a republic.

2

THE REPUBLIC

The Latin term *res publica* (from which comes the word 'republic') is usually translated as 'state' or 'commonwealth'. At no time was Rome a democracy (that is rule by the people) in the Greek, or true, sense. Its society was rigidly divided by legal status (free or enslaved) and by class. Free men or women were further classified, for example, according to whether they were so by birth or by release from slavery, were Roman citizens or Latins, or were independent or answerable to a guardian or other person in authority. The republic began, and finished, as a state largely dominated by the two upper classes, the senators, who qualified by birth and wealth, and the equestrians or knights, those in the second of the five categories to which people were allotted according to their means; until the second century BC, the latter were, by reason of their property holding, provided at public expense with a horse, with which they were required to report for military duty. The constitutional change from monarchy to republic was gradual. The main functions of the king, including full military command, were undertaken by two consuls with equal powers, elected for one year only. '[Lucius Valerius] Publicola [one of the original consuls] instituted the rule that the lictors should march in front of each consul on alternate months, so that the insignia of office should not be more numerous in the republic than under the kings' (Cicero, *On the Republic*, II. 31).

From 367 BC, one consulship was normally held by a plebeian, though by this time consular duties were mainly formal: according to Varro, 'the consul was so named because he "consults" the people and the senate' (*On the Latin Language*, V. 14). The constitution allowed, however, that in time of crisis, and particularly

13

in war, a single 'dictator' could be nominated who would exercise complete control for not more than six months. This was an ancient office whose origins lay in the appointment of one commander over the armies of several Latin city states. He was called 'master of the infantry', and even in republican times his second-in-command was called 'master of the cavalry'.

In 356 BC, Gaius Marcius Rutilus became the first plebeian dictator, in charge of operations against a combined Etruscan force which had advanced into Roman territory as far as the ancient salt-works on the coast. The patricians put all sorts of difficulties in his way, but he marched his army out of the city, put it across the Tiber on rafts, captured the enemy camp by surprise, took 8,000 prisoners, and killed or drove away the rest. On his return the patrician-dominated senate denied him the statutory triumphal procession which he had earned, but the people took no notice and gave him his triumph all the same.

Matters of state religion were in the hands of the *pontifex maximus* (high priest) – the literal meaning of *pontifex* is 'bridge builder'. This was an elected office, in the same way as those of other state officials, but with it in his case went an official residence in the middle of the forum. The *pontifex maximus* was responsible for the calendar, for presiding at state ceremonies, and for the nomination of vestal virgins and some priests. He also had disciplinary powers over the priestly classes.

As the tasks of government of state and empire grew, so other political offices were created.

Censor (Two): chief registrar, financial and tax officer, inspector of public works, and arbiter of public morality:

> Censors shall list all citizens, recording their age, antece-
> dents, families, and means. They shall supervise the city's
> temples, roads, water system, treasury, and revenues. They
> shall divide citizens into tribes, and list them also according
> to wealth, age, and rank. They shall assign young men to the
> cavalry and infantry. They shall discourage the unmarried
> state, guard public morality, and suspend from the senate
> anyone guilty of improper conduct.
>
> (Cicero, *On the Laws*, III. 3)

The office was instituted in 444 BC; the first plebeian to hold it was Gaius Marcius Rutilus in 351 BC. The post was usually

Figure 3   The early Roman coinage in certain respects still followed the principle established under the kings of currency being linked to weight. This *aes grave* (heavy bronze) *dupondius* (*c.* 265 BC) is worth 2 *asses* (represented by the two bars) and carries the head of Roma, the personification of the city. (Actual size)

restricted to those who had climbed the 'ladder of honour' from quaestor to consul. From the second century BC elections took place every five years, to coincide with the taking of the census of the people. A censor held office for only eighteen months, though his acts remained in force until the next election. He had wide disciplinary powers.

> Anyone who let his land grow wild and was not giving it enough attention, or had not ploughed it or weeded it, or had neglected his orchard or vineyard, did not go unpunished. It became a matter for the censors, who would reduce him to the lowest rank of citizen. In the same way, a knight whose horse looked skinny or was badly turned out was charged with negligence.
>
> (Aulus Gellius, *Attic Nights*, IV. 12)

15

Praetor (Six after 197 BC): chief law officer and judge, and understudy to the consuls, particularly in the administration of provinces (provincial governors were normally drawn from the ranks of former consuls and serving or former praetors). The first praetor was in 366 BC; about a century later a second was appointed, the two dividing their responsibility for justice according to whether a suit was between citizens or outsiders. The first plebeian praetor was in 337 BC.

Aedile (Four after 366 BC): supervisor of public works, temples, markets, and games. Two at least were always plebeians.

Quaestor (Four after 421 BC, ten after 267 BC): assistant to the consuls, particularly as a controller of the military or the civic treasury, and keeper of records. The minimum age was 25, to allow for the completion of military service. The first plebeian quaestor was in 409 BC.

While the existence of the various assemblies gives the Roman constitution an air of democracy, the senate was officially an advisory body, and in none of the others did members vote as individuals. Voting was by group or category according to the assembly's composition; the majority voice of a group represented a single vote. State officials (*magistri*) were elected by this means.

Senate: about 300 members up to the reforms of Sulla. Nominations were originally automatic and by birth or rank; later they were made by the consuls and, after about 350 BC, by the censors. Plebeians were admitted during the fourth century BC, after which the senate became a body predominantly of men who had served as government officials. It did not pass laws so much as refer its advice (*senatus consultum*) to the popular assemblies. It had, however, complete control over finance, administration of the state and its empire, and relations with foreign powers. It also adjudicated on religious matters and acted as an intermediary between the the Roman people and the gods.

Comitia curiata: an assembly of representatives of wards, ten each from the three original tribes of Rome, which was the original people's council at the time of the kings. It formally ratified the election of consuls and acted as a court of appeal. In the fourth century BC its functions were largely assumed by the *comitia centuriata*.

Comitia centuriata: originally the assembly of representatives of military units (centuries). It was reconstituted in 193 centuries, to which eligible voters (all Roman citizens) were allocated according to their means, eighty-eight of the votes being distributed among those in the top two property bands. It was reorganized in about 200 BC to give slightly more influence to those in the three less well-off classes, who represented the majority of the people. The assembly elected senior state officials, declared war, instituted peace treaties, approved legislation, and, until the function was completely transferred to the courts, had the final say in cases of execution or exile.

Concilium plebis (meeting of the people): the original plebeian parliament, sitting and voting in thirty-five tribal or district divisions. It elected its own officers and formulated decrees (*plebiscita*) for observance by its own kind which, after 287 BC, could be made binding on the whole community.

Comitia tributa (tribal assembly): organized in tribes in the same way as the *concilium plebis* but open to all citizens. It elected minor officials and was a means of approving legislation on a different voting basis to that of the *comitia centuriata*.

At the outset of the republic, the patricians had not only the means and inclination to exercise government, but all the power as well. The bid by the *plebs* for rights with which to improve their lot was accompanied neither by revolution nor violence, but by passive resistance and collective bargaining. One major concession was the creation in about 494 BC of the office of *tribunus plebis* (tribune of the people), to be a convenor of the popular assemblies and to present the people's grievances to the consuls or senate. A tribune had extraordinary powers. Whereas a government official could quash an act of a colleague of equal status, a tribune of the people could hold up almost any business of state, including actions of officials and resolutions of the senate, merely by pronouncing a veto. He was required to be on call day and night, to any citizen who required help. Cicero

17

(106–43 BC), who was an equestrian by birth, describes the initial process of change in one of his political dialogues:

> Quite soon, in the sixteenth year of the republic, something happened which by the nature of things was inevitable: the people, freed from the rule of kings, claimed rather more rights for themselves. There was perhaps some justification for this, yet often it is in the very nature of a republic to contradict the justifiable. Remember what I said at the beginning: unless a state maintains a balance of rights, duties, and functions, so that state officials possess enough power, deliberations of the leading citizens enough authority, and the people enough freedom, it is not possible for it to remain stable. At a time when the community was in financial difficulties, the *plebs* occupied first the Sacred Mount [5 km outside the city], and then the Aventine Hill itself. Just as the disciplinary measures of Lycurgus could not keep even Greek citizens in check, and in Sparta in the reign of Theopompus five officers called ephors and in Crete ten cosmoi were appointed to act as opposition to the monarchy, so the *plebs* elected its own tribunes to represent its rights in the face of the power of the consuls.
>
> (*On the Republic*, II. 33)

THE TWELVE TABLES

Another significant development was the appointment in 451 BC of the *decemviri*, a committee of ten, to refine, standardize, and record a statutory code of law. The result, known as the Twelve Tables, was engraved in copper and permanently displayed to public view. Infuriatingly enough, and perhaps largely because these laws became so well known that three centuries later schoolboys were required to chant them in class by rote, only a few fragments and references survive. They clearly constituted, however, a condensed set of rules for public, private, and political behaviour, covering in each case a variety of circumstances within a precise format.

Thus, if a defendant in a civil case refused to appear in court, the plaintiff could apply physical force to get him there; if the defendant was too old or ill to attend, the plaintiff must provide transport. Anyone caught stealing at night could lawfully be killed by the owner of the property. By day, other regulations applied. If the thief was a freeman, he was to be flogged and bound over to the injured party; if a slave, flogged and thrown over the Tarpeian Rock; if under the age of puberty, flogged and required to make reparation.

There were laws governing hygiene and fire-risk (no burials or cremations within the city limits), and the upkeep of roads (the responsibility of those on whose property they bordered). There was a statutory maximum rate of interest on loans. Anyone confessing or adjudged to be a debtor had thirty days in which to pay; after that he could be sold into slavery by his creditors or, according to Aulus Gellius (c. AD 123–c. 169), philosopher and antiquarian, carved up into proportionate pieces. There was a fixed penalty for assault (with a reduction if the victim was a slave). Stealing crops was a capital offence: so was slander (by clubbing to death). We do not know what penalty was prescribed for murder, only that according to Pliny the Elder it was lighter than for stealing crops. There was a distinction between intentional and accidental homicide: Cicero illustrated it by comparing a javelin which has been aimed to one which has simply 'slipped from the hand' (*Topica*, XVII. 64). It was a criminal offence to cast a spell on anyone by incantation or to demonstrate in the streets against an individual. You could remove any parts of your neighbour's tree which overhung your property. And a father had the right to kill his deformed child.

Even more important than the actual details – and the laws contained in the Twelve Tables were never formally repealed in Roman times – was the fact that now everyone, patrician, plebeian, consul, senator, state official, ordinary citizen, was subject to the same written code, professionally drafted and precisely stated in terms which demonstrate the Roman aptitude for legal expression and constitute the starting point of European as well as of Roman law.

According to the historian Livy (59 BC–AD 17), the *decemviri* themselves came to sticky ends. The committee's chairman, Appius Claudius, lusted after Virginia, the daughter of a centurion. When she resisted his advances, he got one of his lackeys to claim she was his slave. When the matter came to court, Appius was the judge who pronounced against her; whereupon Virginia's father, preferring her death to her dishonour, killed her with his sword. At this point the tribune of the people took a hand, and Appius himself was remanded in custody, where he committed suicide rather than face trial. Another *decemvir* also killed himself, and the rest, who had refused to give up their offices at the end of their statutory year's appointment and were alleged to have used their self-assumed judicial authority to commit crimes, were exiled and their property was confiscated.

Corruption in high places, and the corruption that is fostered by power itself, was neither a Roman prerogative nor a Roman invention. The system did, however, allow some dedicated idealists and radicals genuinely to make felt their attempts to reform aspects of the constitution and to break down the prevailing dichotomy between rich and poor.

FROM CITY STATE TO ITALIAN EMPIRE

By 265 BC the Romans had conquered the whole of the Italian peninsula below the river Arno, by a process that was more like explosion than expansion. They also successfully resisted several incursions into their territory by the Gauls who occupied the Po valley, and in 275 BC had finally seen off the hired army under Pyrrhus (318–272 BC), king of Epirus, who had been called in by Tarentum to protect its own interests and those of other Greek city states in the south. This was a fine achievement, over a Greek army which was organized and which fought in the style and tradition of Alexander the Great, and against the foremost general of the time. To him we owe the term 'Pyrrhic victory'. After defeating the Romans at Heraclea in 280 BC by the ingenious deployment of his elephant corps but otherwise at considerable cost to his own forces, he is reported as remarking that one more victory like that against the Romans and he would be finished! According to Plutarch, he died during an assault on Argos, after an old woman, seeing him engaged in hand-to-hand combat with her son, hurled a roof tile at him, and scored a direct hit.

The attitude of the Romans to the peoples they defeated was enlightened and tactically sound. They refused to deal with conglomerates of states, such as the league of Latin cities to which Rome had originally belonged, or with the Etruscan empire as a whole. They insisted on treating each conquest on its individual merits, and imposed restrictions or awarded privileges according to the circumstances. Some were granted

Roman citizenship without voting rights, and some a kind of probationary citizenship; others had to give up part of their territory, which became public land or was carved up into lots for the use of Roman citizens, or employed as the site for a new colony. Defeated states were sometimes allowed the right of trade and intermarriage with Rome, but never with each other – it was a case of applying in practical terms the Roman proverb 'divide and rule'. All were required regularly to provide manpower for the armies of Rome. This continuous supply of recruits was a factor in the determination to extend the power of Rome. It was not until the second century BC that soldiers received any formal pay, though from 406 BC they were reimbursed for their field expenses, less the cost of rations and other items from the military stores. A soldier's reward was in spoils and land: the Roman empire grew as a means of providing these.

A crucial date in the Romanization of Italy was 338 BC. This marked the final capitulation and dissolution of the Latin league of states, and the establishment of Roman colonies along the coast of Latium which were out of bounds to settlers from other Latin towns. Shortly afterwards, treaties were made with the important Campanian towns of Cumae and Capua, originally of Greek foundation but more recently under Etruscan domination, whereby these, and certain other communities in the region, accepted a form of Roman citizenship and the duty of supplying soldiers in return for a promise of military protection.

It was not long before the call for protection came, against the Samnite invasions of Campania. The Samnites were a different proposition from any enemy of Rome so far. They could be contained quite easily on the plains of central Italy, but once they retired to their mountainous homelands new military tactics were required to dislodge them. The war lasted with few interruptions for thirty-seven years until 290 BC. It culminated in predictable victory for the Romans, but not before they had, in 321 BC, suffered the most shameful defeat in their history. Trapped in the Caudine Forks, a series of narrow mountain passes, the whole Roman army, with its consuls and officers, was forced to surrender. Six hundred knights were demanded and handed over as hostages. Then the real humiliation began.

The lictors were ordered to stand aside from the consuls, who were stripped of their cloaks of office. This so affected

21

the ranks, who only a short time before had cursed them and called for them to be tortured, that each man, ignoring his own situation, averted his eyes from the degradation of such high office as though from an unspeakable horror.

First the consuls, half naked, suffered the ignominious ordeal of being sent under the yoke. They were followed by their officers, in descending order of rank, then, one after the other, by the legions themselves, while the enemy, fully armed, stood round, hurling insults and cracking jokes. Many had swords brandished in their faces, and some, whose attitude of indignation at their treatment offended their captors, were maimed or killed.

So they went under the yoke: almost the worst thing about it was being watched by their enemies. When they emerged from the pass, though their appearance was of men back from the grave first seeing the light of day, as they looked around at the ghastly procession the light itself seemed grimmer than any death.

(Livy, *History of Rome*, IX. 5, 6)

The last-remaining Etruscan footholds in Campania had been swept away in the latter part of the fifth century during incursions by Oscan-speaking tribes from the southern Apennines. The disintegration of the rest of the Etruscan empire was begun in 310 BC when a Roman army not only penetrated as far as the wooded slopes of Mount Ciminius, but by a forced march through the forest got behind the opposing confederate army and crushed it. Three major Etruscan cities immediately sued for peace. The rest followed suit by degrees until 283 BC, when the capitulation was complete.

The Gaulish tribes who had spilled over into the fertile valley of the Po as a result of Celtic migrations in the fifth century BC resisted Roman attempts to annex their territory until 191 BC, and though Ligurian tribes on the east coast offered pockets of resistance for a further twenty years, the whole region now recognized as Italy was soon in Roman hands.

CATO THE CENSOR (234–149 BC)

The progress from quaestor to consul via the offices of aedile and praetor was a natural one, and came more quickly to those

22

who had proved themselves able soldiers in time of war. On the other hand, as under normal circumstances no one could hold the same office twice in ten years, unless there was a suitable provincial governorship available, some very accomplished men could be left without full-time employment at the height of their powers. Such a one was Marcus Porcius Cato, also known as Cato the Elder to distinguish him from his great-grandson, Marcus Porcius Cato 'of Utica' (95–46 BC), a political leader of the utmost integrity and single-mindedness. Cato senior was born at Tusculum and brought up there on his father's farm. He first saw army service when he was 17. He was consul in 195 BC – he led his forces to a great victory in Spain – and retired from the army in 191 BC after a distinguished military career. As a senator he participated enthusiastically in debates on civil affairs; in 184 BC he stood for and was elected to the office of censor.

Cato took his duties as guardian of public morals very seriously.

> He expelled Manilius, a prospective candidate for the con-
> sulship, from the senate for embracing his wife during the
> day in front of their daughter. For himself, he said that he
> never embraced his own wife except when it thundered
> loudly, adding jocularly that he was delighted when it *did*
> happen to thunder.
>
> (Plutarch, *Lives: Cato*, XVII. 7)

He could be ruthless and implacable with his enemies, especially when they were members of the urban aristocracy, which he was not, and strenuous in his pursuit of those who misused public property. He cut off the pipes by which people were in the habit of siphoning off part of the municipal water supply into their own houses and gardens, and knocked down private buildings which encroached on to public land. He imposed taxes on the rich, and even heavier taxes on the very rich, and introduced police regulations to restrict luxurious living and entertaining. He was hated for his rural ways, his harshness, his outspokenness, and his parsimony, but he was respected as a skilled politician and a persuasive public speaker. Thus it was that in his last political act, as a senator of 85, he was able to initiate a war that ultimately resulted in the destruction of a whole civilization, as we shall see.

He never properly retired from active life. He compiled the earliest Roman encyclopaedia, and wrote a medical work, a history of Rome, and a treatise on agriculture. The latter, the only book of his that we have, is the oldest surviving complete prose work in Latin. It is revealing of its author and the times in that it extols not so much the glories and virtues of drawing on the bounties of the land, as the pursuit of cash-farming as a less perilous investment than commerce. Its approach is practical, traditional, and often picturesque.

> *When it rains*: Look for what can be done under cover. Don't stop work, clean up. Remember, even if there is nothing to do, expenses still mount up. . . .
> *To make green olive oil*: Collect windfalls as soon as possible; if they are soiled, wash them and remove any leaves and dirt. Pick olives when they are black. Oil made from sourest olives is the best. The most profitable oil is from ripe olives. If they have been touched by frost, press the oil three or four days after picking; if you want, add salt to them. . . .
> *For snake bite*: If an ox or any other animal has been bitten by a snake, mix a cup of ground fennel (doctors call it camomile) into a pint of old wine. Administer through the nostrils and apply pig's dung to the bite itself. Treat a person in the same way, if the situation arises. . . .
> *The properties of cabbage*: Cabbage is a marvellous digestive and an excellent laxative; after you have eaten it, your urine will relieve all complaints. If you want to gorge yourself at a party and imbibe freely, before you go eat as much pickled cabbage as you need, and when you get home chew about five raw leaves of the stuff. You will feel as though you have eaten nothing, and you can drink as much as you like.
> (*On Agriculture*, XXXIX, LXV, CII, CLVI)

A fervent nationalist, Cato was ambivalent towards Greek culture. He professed himself averse to Greek philosophers and doctors, and claimed that Greek literature was worth only a passing glance. From what we know of his speeches and writings, however, and from the observations of his contemporary, the Greek historian Polybius (*c.* 202–120 BC), it is clear that he was steeped in Greek rhetorical theory and literary tradition.

THE PUNIC WARS (264–146 BC)

The spark which ignited the metamorphosis of Rome from an Italian to a Mediterranean power was a small enough incident. The Greek city of Messana, on the north-eastern tip of Sicily, had in 289 BC been seized and occupied by a notorious gang of retired Campanian mercenaries. They were still there in 264 BC, when the king of Syracuse, the famous Greek stronghold lower down the coast, decided to winkle them out. The mercenaries asked the Carthaginians, who occupied parts of the west coast of Sicily, to send a fleet and raise the siege. The Carthaginians duly obliged, but their fleet stayed on in the harbour. The mercenaries then appealed to Rome to rid them of the Carthaginians, on the somewhat specious grounds that their Campanian blood entitled them to the same protection as the Campanian allies of Rome on the mainland. The senate havered and passed the buck to the *comitia tributa*, which voted if not actually for war, then at least for the dispatch of an expedition against the interfering Carthaginians to restore Messana to its criminal element. The arrival of the expedition so surprised or unnerved the Carthaginian commander at Messana that he embarked and took his ships home. The Carthaginian government, however, humiliated by what they saw as a defeat, resolved to recapture Messana.

Figure 4 Part of a relief, dating most probably from the time of the Second Punic War, depicting the traditional sacrifice to Mars, god of war, of a bull, a sheep, and a pig. The soldiers on the right, standing at ease, are wearing mail shirts, later replaced by the *lorica segmentata*, a flexible corselet of overlapping strips of iron attached to leather thongs. (*Louvre*)

25

Thus was started, by accident, the first world war in history to be contested on principles. It was fought to the finish, and to the death. It lasted, in three 'bites' totalling forty-two years, for well over a century. When it ended, Carthage, which at one time had, according to the Greek geographer Strabo (*c.* 64 BC–AD 19), '300 cities in Libya and 700 thousand people in its own city' (*Geography*, XVII. 3), was a smoking heap of rubble.

Carthage was originally a Phoenician colony: hence the Latin name for a Carthaginian, *Poenus*, from which comes the adjective 'Punic'. The language of the Carthaginians was Semitic, and their gods, too, were those of the Phoenicians, notably Ba'al-Hammon, god of the sky and of fertility, and Tanit, the moon-goddess. Its literature has not come down to us. The Punic Wars went on for so long and were fought with such intensity on both sides that within a hundred years the word *punicus* had an accepted literary meaning of 'treacherous', though, while hostilities were conducted with the utmost passion and brutality, there is no evidence that either side acted more dishonestly than the other.

The Carthaginians can justly be called one of the most successful peoples of the ancient world. Virgil refers to their city as 'opposite Italy and the mouths of the Tiber, rich in resources and especially severe in the pursuit of war' (*Aeneid*, I. 13–14). It was this key strategic position in the Mediterranean which governed their military tactics and, in turn, their economic policy. Carthage was a sea-going nation, using its fleet, which was manned by its citizens, virtually to close the western Mediterranean to other nations, to wage war, and to trade in goods all round the Mediterranean and down the west coast of Africa as far as Guinea – gold, ivory, bronze, tin, pottery, grain, perfume, dyes, and, of course, slaves. It founded colonies along the North African coast as far as Cyrenaica, in southern Spain, in Corsica, Sardinia, and on the western tip of Sicily. Carthaginian citizens did not normally fight in the army, which was composed mainly of African conscripts and mercenaries from all parts of the Mediterranean – and Carthage could afford to employ the best. This multi-racial army still had to be forged into a coherent fighting force, which was the responsibility of its commanders, who were Carthaginians and professional career soldiers.

The First Punic War (264–241 BC) was largely fought at sea.

The Romans purpose-built a series of fleets to match the Carthaginian numbers and manned them with marine commandos trained in hand-to-hand fighting – in an age of rudimentary artillery, the standard naval tactic was to attach grapples to an enemy ship and then overwhelm its crew by superior numbers. The losses on both sides were enormous, but the Romans were better at unearthing and deploying ever more resources, and finally the Carthaginians sued for peace and agreed to withdraw all claims to Sicily. Shortly after hostilities ceased, however, the Romans took advantage of the temporary preoccupation of the Carthaginians with a revolt of their mercenaries to annex Corsica and Sardinia, an act which was undeniably foul play.

Carthage retaliated by increasing its empire in another quarter: the whole of southern Spain, with its potential wealth and manpower, was overrun. This Spanish campaign was led successively by a brilliant family trio of generals: Hamilcar (d. 229 BC), his son-in-law Hasdrubal (d. 221 BC), and Hamilcar's son Hannibal (247–182 BC). It was so successful that in order to prevent Carthage extending its influence still farther north, the Romans were forced into a diplomatic manoeuvre. The river Ebro was to be regarded as the boundary between the interests of the two sides, but the town of Saguntum on the east coast would remain nominally under Roman protection. When in 221 BC Hasdrubal was murdered by a slave whose master he had put to death, Hannibal succeeded to the command. He started the Second Punic War (218–202 BC) by attacking and capturing Saguntum. This was clearly a deliberate ploy. The Carthaginians were motivated to set up this new confrontation by a desire for revenge and by their fear of Roman incursions into their newly-won territory.

The Romans began by assuming that tactically this war would be a continuation of the first, and prepared a fleet in which they could cross to Carthage and this time take the city itself. Hannibal confounded them (and the rest of the world then and since) by doing not just the unexpected, but the impossible. He marched his army – infantry, cavalry, baggage train, and heavy tanks in the form of his famous elephants – out of Spain and across the river Rhône on a flotilla of boats and rafts, against continual opposition from native Gallic tribes. He invaded Italy by a route which took him over, and through, the Alps; at one point he had to blast away a wall of solid rock by heating it with fires and then dashing on to it quantities of raw wine. According to Polybius, who is regarded as the most reliable authority, Hannibal entered Italy with 20,000 foot and 6,000 cavalry, having lost 18,000 infantry and 2,000 horsemen since crossing the Rhône. With these, and the surviving elephants, he soon gained control of northern Italy, having outflanked one Roman army before the river Trebia, and trapped another by Lake Trasimene. Rome itself was too tough a nut to crack, so Hannibal bypassed the city and went on into the south, where at Cannae he outmanoeuvred a numerically much stronger Roman force and virtually annihilated it. Then for fourteen years he and his army rampaged around southern Italy before being lured back to Carthage, and to defeat at Zama in 202 BC, by a splendid African campaign conducted by Cornelius Scipio (234–183 BC), who had already driven the Carthaginians out of Spain and was afterwards awarded the honorific surname of Africanus. In particular, he managed at Zama to neutralize Hannibal's tactics of opening the battle with a frontal charge of his eighty elephants. Hannibal survived the battle, only to end his life in exile in Asia, having failed in his attempt to rebuild his country's fortunes by political means.

As a man, Hannibal was 'notorious in Carthaginian circles for his love of money, and among the Romans for his cruelty' (Polybius, *Histories*, IX. 26). As a soldier, Hannibal is just one of a line of gallant and spectacular commanders whose efforts finally ended in failure but whose exploits are remembered better than, or at least as well as, those of the men who ultimately defeated them: Leonidas of Sparta, Spartacus the gladiator, Saladin, Montrose, Napoleon, Custer, and Rommel are others. Scipio Africanus was the equal in the field of that most renowned of Roman generals, Julius Caesar. Livy has a neat story of how Scipio and Hannibal met again in Ephesus in 193 BC. He claims it originated with Acilius, a senator who was writing in Greek not long after the meeting was supposed to have taken place. The conversation went like this:

SCIPIO:	Who do you think was the greatest army commander of all?
HANNIBAL:	Alexander, because time and again he overwhelmed armies with a tiny force of his own, and marched right

	through regions of the world farther away than anyone had ever expected even to see.
SCIPIO:	And after him?
HANNIBAL:	Pyrrhus, for being the first to teach the art of making a proper camp, for choosing his ground and arranging his defences better than anyone else, and for his quality of leadership, which enabled him to persuade Italian races to accept his command, that of a foreign king, rather than Rome's, which had been predominant for so long.
SCIPIO:	And third?
HANNIBAL:	Why, myself!
SCIPIO (*Laughing*):	What would you have said if you had beaten me?
HANNIBAL:	Then without question I'd put myself ahead of Alexander and Pyrrhus and all other generals.

(History of Rome, XXXV. 14)

After the Second Punic War, Rome confiscated Spain, leaving Carthage with just its north African colonies, and promptly waded into local Spanish conflicts to keep the tribes there in order, besides being involved in full-scale wars in Macedonia, Asia Minor, and Syria. In spite of the sanctions and conditions of peace that had been imposed on Carthage at the end of the war, there was the possibility that it might rise again and try to take revenge on its conquerors. Old Cato, who in 157 BC had been a member of a diplomatic mission to Africa to mediate between Carthage and neighbouring Numidia, saw this more clearly than anyone else.

It is said that he even contrived to drop a Libyan fig on the floor of the senate as he rearranged his toga. Then, as the rest admired its size and lusciousness, he warned them that the land where it grew was only three days away from Rome by sea. In another respect, he was even more uncompromising. Whatever question was being addressed in the senate, he incorporated into his speech the words, 'In my opinion, Carthage must be destroyed.'

(Plutarch, *Lives: Cato*, XXVII)

The Carthaginians were finally manoeuvred into the position of having to defend themselves against Numidian invasions of their territory. This was technically a breach of the treaty of 201 BC, under which they were forbidden to take up arms without Rome's permission. The senate, which, egged on by Cato, had made plans for just such an eventuality, voted for war once again. They sent out a trained army comprising, according to the Alexandrian Greek historian Appian (*c.* AD 95–*c.* 165), 80,000 infantry and 4,000 cavalry, under the command of the consuls, 'to whom they gave secret orders not to discontinue the war until Carthage had been razed to the ground' (*Punic Wars*, VIII. 11). The Third Punic War lasted for just three years (149–146 BC). That it continued so long was due to a heroic Carthaginian defence of their city. It was hastily mounted, since the messenger who brought the news of the senate's declaration of war also carried the announcement that the expeditionary force had sailed. It was, too, frenziedly maintained, since as part of the conditions of the surrender of the city at the end of the previous war the Carthaginians had handed over '200,000 full suits of armour and 3,000 anti-siege engines as sureties against their going to war again' (Strabo, *Geography*, XVII. 3). Carthage was duly destroyed. The 50,000 survivors of the siege were sold into slavery.

TIBERIUS GRACCHUS (168–133 BC) AND GAIUS GRACCHUS (*c.* 159–121 BC)

To have as father a famous consul and military leader, and as mother a Scipio (one of the most distinguished of all the patrician families) who, when widowed and faced with bringing up twelve children, turned down an offer of marriage from the king of Egypt, are unusual antecedents of two men whose political reforms and championship of the poor and needy did most to upset the established order in republican Rome. Yet, if there may have been no precedent for such a response to an aristocratic upbringing, there have been many examples since.

In the same way as all young men of his social class, Tiberius

30

Sempronius Gracchus served in the army. This he did with considerable distinction, and was elected quaestor. In a campaign against Numantia in Spain, his instinctive political bent involved him in negotiations with the enemy to save the Roman army from annihilation. His efforts were successful, for he saved the lives of 20,000 Romans and countless auxiliaries and camp followers (and had his accounts' books returned to him by the enemy), but the surrender did not go down well at home. Largely thanks to the intervention of his brother-in-law, yet another notable member of the Scipio clan, Tiberius and his fellow-officers avoided any further indignity, but their commanding officer was stripped, put in irons, and returned to the enemy who had originally spared him.

Tiberius then turned to politics and was elected a tribune of the people for 133 BC. The main reform he proposed was the reclamation of large tracts of land which had been acquired by the state in its conquest of Italy, and its redistribution among smallholders with guaranteed tenure in return for a nominal rent. Those currently occupying the land, who were in fact merely tenants of the state, would be restricted to what had for some time been the legal limit of ownership (300 acres plus a further 250 acres for each of up to two sons), and would be compensated by being granted a hereditary rent-free lease.

He did not draft his law on his own, but consulted leading citizens who were noted for their uprightness, among them Crassus the *pontifex maximus*, Mucius Scaevola the legal expert, who was consul at the time, and Appius Claudius, his own father-in-law. And it is considered that a law against injustice and greed has never been expressed in such mild and diplomatic terms. For men who should have submitted to the process of law for disobeying it, and been fined and deprived of the land which they occupied illegally, were instead merely required to give up their unjust holdings in return for fair recompense, and to allow them to be taken over by needy citizens.

(Plutarch, *Lives: Tiberius Gracchus*, V)

It was a significant political package at a time of general unrest and of expansion abroad in that it also restored to the list of those eligible for military service (for which a tradition of qualification was the possession of land) a section of society which had fallen out of the reckoning.

Though the bill had the backing of several prominent members of the senate as well as of one of the consuls, Tiberius's tactics in trying to make it law were questionable. Instead of submitting it first for discussion in the senate, he proposed it straight to the *comitia tributa*, where it was bound to succeed. This inevitably annoyed the senate, which persuaded one of the other tribunes to veto the bill as it was being read out. Tiberius retaliated by invoking his right to suspend all business. He then refused to listen to attempts to get him to refer the bill to the senate, and took the unprecedented step of asking the *comitia tributa* to vote his refractory colleague out of office, which it promptly did. The bill was then passed to acclamation, and three commissioners were appointed to administer the scheme: Tiberius himself, his younger brother Gaius Sempronius Gracchus, and Appius Claudius Pulcher, 'leader' of the senate as well as being Tiberius's father-in-law.

The commission immediately began work, and in all about 75,000 smallholdings may have been created and farmed as a result. When it began to look as though the commission would run short of funds, Tiberius coolly proposed to the *comitia tributa* that the revenue confiscated from the newly acquired kingdom of Pergamum should be diverted to its use. The senate, rather than risk being outflanked again, and this time in the area of finance, which it regarded as its prerogative, capitulated, but Tiberius was a marked man. State officials could not be brought to task while in office, but they could be prosecuted afterwards for acts committed during their term. Tiberius Gracchus now took the unprecedented and arguably unconstitutional step of announcing himself as a candidate for a tribuneship for a second year running. A group of senators, failing in an attempt to have him disqualified from standing, charged out of the senate, broke up an electioneering meeting which Tiberius was addressing, and clubbed him to death with stools and cudgels.

They had not by any means heard the last of the Gracchus family. Nine years after his brother's assassination, Gaius Sempronius Gracchus was elected a tribune of the people. He was elected again, unopposed, the following year – there is some suggestion that one of his first acts in office was to have the law repealed whereby a man could not hold office for two years running. Gaius was a different and more formidable proposition than Tiberius. He was more flamboyant and passionate, and a skilled and powerful demagogue. His programme of reforms passed by the *comitia tributa* was wide-ranging and designed to benefit all interests, except of course those of the senate. He reaffirmed and reactivated his brother's land laws and established smallholdings in Roman territory abroad. For city-dwellers who could not be persuaded to leave the teeming streets of Rome for the hazards of country life, he enacted corn laws which entitled every citizen on demand to a monthly ration at a fixed price. While the nobility still dominated the senate, the wealth and business acumen lay largely with the equestrian class. Gaius Gracchus gave them greater power, and riches, by awarding them the right to contract for gathering the enormous taxes which accrued from the newly created province of Asia, and by substituting knights for senators as jurors in cases of extortion brought by the state against provincial governors. He also forced through massive measures for expenditure on public works, particularly roads and harbours, which again benefited the business community. His most enlightened piece of legislation, however, fell foul even of the *comitia tributa*. This was a proposal to extend full Roman citizenship, and thus voting rights, to the population of the surrounding area of Latium, and to give all allied states in Italy the rights enjoyed by the Latins, such as trade with Rome and intermarriage with Romans.

When Gaius Gracchus offered himself in 121 BC for a third term of office as tribune, the senate resorted to terrorism once again, though this time with quasi-constitutional overtones. They put up against him a straw candidate with an entirely fallacious programme of reforms which would be even more acceptable to the people, who was duly elected. The supporters of Gaius Gracchus held a mass rally on the Aventine Hill, but made the mistake of carrying weapons. The consul, Lucius Opimius, armed with a *senatus consultum ultimum*, which gave moral backing to a senior official to take action against those who were endangering the stability of the state, raised a levy of citizens, augmented by a company of soldiers and archers, to disperse the demonstrators. Gaius escaped the first wave of violence, but then, recognizing that the cause was hopeless, ordered his personal slave to stab him to death. It is said that

3,000 of his supporters were rounded up and thrown into jail, and there strangled.

The actions and ultimate fates of the brothers Gracchus constituted a watershed in Roman politics. Their legislation highlighted the links between the problems of property holding, poverty, the army, and the extension and retention of the empire. Their use of a popular assembly to initiate legislation gave it powers rivalling those of the senate. That political conflict could lead twice to violence established a precedent which affected the equilibrium of Roman society and instigated periods of anarchy and civil war.

GAIUS MARIUS (157–86 BC) AND THE REFORM OF THE ROMAN ARMY

For an inherently agricultural society to be a perpetual war machine is to attempt to mix two incompatibles. The soil and climate of the Italian peninsula offered its inhabitants means of personal survival and economic development which were not available on a similar scale to any other society of the ancient world. The geographical situation, however, of early Rome, hemmed in by inimical or potentially inimical tribes, meant that its survival depended not so much on defence as on aggression. What Tiberius Gracchus tried to halt when he was tribune in 133 BC was a trend which had begun centuries earlier and which, by the very success with which Rome had conducted its military operations, had become a vicious circle. Ancient armies were manned by peasant farmers. A society continually at war required a constant supply of conscripts. Smallholdings fell into disuse because there was no one to tend them. As Roman conquests spread through the Mediterranean lands, even more men were required, and wealth and cheap corn poured back into Rome, much of it into the hands of entrepreneurs, who became even richer and invested in land out of which they carved vast areas for vegetables, vines, olives, and sheep farming, all managed by slave labour. The dispossessed rural poor became the urban poor, thus also becoming ineligible for military service as no longer being nominal property holders. Not only was there a shortage of recruits, but the soldier had nothing to return to between campaigns or at the end of his service.

A working solution to the problem of recruitment was devised by Gaius Marius, a man of humble origins who was born near Arpinum, a town in Latium about 100 km from Rome but not far off the main road to Capua, the Via Latina. He first saw military service in Spain, and did not hold any public office until he was 38, when he was elected tribune of the people. Four years later, in 115 BC, he managed to achieve a praetorship and made a good marriage, to Julia of the family of that name; he was thus to become an uncle by marriage of Julius Caesar. He then served in the African wars against Jugurtha, who in the wake of the destruction of Carthage had usurped the whole of Numidia after being granted half of it. Marius returned to Rome in 108 BC to stand successfully for consul, in which capacity the *comitia tributa* elected him to assume military command in Africa, an infringement of the traditional prerogative of the senate to make military appointments. Abandoning the usual methods of enlisting servicemen, Marius openly recruited volunteers from the ranks of the urban poor, promising them victory, booty, glory, and, of course, permanent jobs. He introduced new training methods and, with the first professional army the Romans ever had, brought the fighting to a speedy end; though the final negotiations, which resulted in the kidnap of Jugurtha and his being handed over to Rome for execution, were conducted by a young quaestor called Cornelius Sulla.

Sallust (86–35 BC), a former member of the senate, quaestor, and proconsular governor of Numidia, who in his retirement became a commentator on recent and contemporary political issues, summed up the situation prevailing in 106–105 BC:

At about this time, our generals Q. Caepio and M. Manlius fought a disastrous battle against the Gauls, which caused general consternation throughout Italy. From that time to this, the Romans have been convinced that other wars were no problem, but when you fought the Gauls, it was for survival, not glory. When the war in Numidia was over, and it was announced that the defeated Jugurtha was being brought back to Rome in chains, Marius was elected consul in his absence and assigned the province of Gaul: as consul he celebrated a magnificent triumph on 1 January. From that time onwards the hopes and prosperity of the state depended on him.

(*The War against Jugurtha*, CXIV)

The Gauls to whom he refers were two displaced Celtic tribes from the north, the Cimbri and Teutones, who in 105 BC, near Arausio (modern Orange), inflicted the greatest defeat on the Romans since Cannae – Caepio and Manlius were later exiled for their incompetence. Marius, having been elected consul for a second term for the year 105 BC, was re-elected for the four successive years 104–101 BC, during which he destroyed the menace of both the Cimbri and the Teutones.

As a professional soldier, at the head of a now professional army, he needed to establish the means for his soldiers to receive allotments of land on discharge and to continue his own career by getting a new command. He threw in his lot with the tribune Lucius Appuleius Saturninus, a man not above using street violence to achieve political ends, with whose help he was elected consul for a sixth time for the year 100 BC. Saturninus now put forward on Marius's behalf a number of legislative proposals in the Gracchus mould, including the usual controversial measures for land allotments to be made to army veterans from the Italian states and full franchise for some of them. The whole programme was accepted, but not without predictable opposition from both nobility and people of Rome which culminated in violent demonstrations. These were put down by Marius's soldiers, who, of course, had a vested interest in the outcome of the debate. This appearance on the streets of Rome of armed military, and their use, without an act of the senate, was a precedent of profound significance. From that time onwards, the rule of Rome was always in the hands of whoever had the support of the army.

The rest of the story of Marius is sheer melodrama. Saturninus instigated the tragic sequence of events by organizing the assassination of an inconvenient political opponent. The senate issued a *senatus consultum ultimum* obliging Marius to take action against his principal supporter, which he did by arresting him with an armed force. An enraged mob then broke into the prison, and lynched Saturninus and several of his cronies. The senate now repealed all Saturninus's laws on the grounds that they had been implemented by force, which was technically true. Marius, left high and dry, with no legislation to back his plans for his soldiers and no political support, went into temporary exile at the end of his year of office.

When he returned, it was to take an active part in the 'Social

War' (91–89 BC). A confederacy of Italian states in the south, fed up with having to fight for Rome without being treated as equals, and not even being allowed to participate in the decisions for which they were fighting, rebelled. They lost the war but eventually gained their objective, most of them being granted full citizenship. In 88 BC all Roman eyes were turned to the east, where Mithridates (*c.* 132–63 BC), king of Pontus, had invaded the Roman province of Asia and massacred 80,000 Roman and Italian citizens. The senate appointed Sulla, who was consul that year, to lead a force against Mithridates. The tribune Sulpicius Rufus (124–88 BC) passed through the *concilium plebis* a package of laws, one of which called for the transfer of this command to Marius. Sulla marched on Rome with his six legions and had the decision reversed. This was the first time that a Roman army had been used against Rome itself.

Sulpicius went into hiding, but was discovered and killed. Marius, now in his seventieth year, fled, accompanied by his adopted son. According to Plutarch, Marius was picked up near the coast of Latium while hiding in a marsh and was sentenced to death by the local magistrates, but was hustled aboard a ship when no one could be found to perform the execution. He ended up in Carthage, but was ordered by the Roman governor in Africa to move on. To the governor's messenger, he replied: 'Go tell your master that you have seen Gaius Marius, a fugitive, sitting in the rubble of Carthage' (Plutarch, *Lives: Marius*, XL).

In the meantime Sulla was carrying out his orders in Asia with some distinction. Cornelius Cinna (d. 84 BC), one of the two consuls for 87 BC, took the opportunity to reintroduce another of the proposals of Sulpicius, the enrolment of the newly enfranchised Italians and also freedmen as members of the traditional thirty-five tribes; he was promptly ejected from the city by his consular colleague. Cinna raised an army of Italian volunteers. He was joined by Marius, now back in Italy with a small force of cavalry, which he augmented by breaking into the quarters in which slaves who worked the farms were held at night and enlisting them as fighting men.

Together Marius and Cinna marched on Rome with their motley army. After a dreadful siege in which thousands died of plague, the government capitulated, having extracted from Cinna a promise that there would be no bloodshed. Marius, who had kept silent during this exchange, obviously did not regard himself as a party to the agreement. The moment the gates were opened, the killing began. It went on for five days. Marius and Cinna then proposed themselves as consuls for the next year, 86 BC. No one dared oppose them. On 13 January, however, Marius died, according to Plutarch of drink and delirium, but possibly simply of old age. He had reformed the army and had been consul an unprecedented seven times, but his ambition, combined with his political naïveté, had caused the stability of authority in Rome to be permanently upset.

SULLA (138–78 BC) AND HIS CONSTITUTIONAL REFORMS

Lucius Cornelius Sulla (surnamed Felix) came of a good family of moderate means. When he returned in 83 BC from his successful eastern campaign, he had no political power beyond that which a man at the head of a trained army of veterans could command. This, however, gave him a more than adequate means of capturing Rome in the face of the nominally more constitutional opposition raised by the consuls, Gnaeus Papirius Carbo (d. 81 BC) and Marius junior (110–82 BC), but not without unnecessary butchery. This accomplished, Sulla then had himself appointed not consul, but dictator. In this capacity his first act was to rid himself of all political and personal opposition, using the novel device of proscription – the posting up of lists of undesirable characters whom anyone was now at liberty to assassinate, and for a reward.

> Sulla himself called the Roman people to assemble, and harangued them with an outburst of self-aggrandisement mixed with menaces intended to put fear into them. . . . He then pronounced sentence of death on forty senators and about 1,600 knights. He seems to have been the first to proscribe those whom he wished murdered, to reward the executioners and informers, and to punish any found hiding the victims. Very soon he added other senators to the list. Some of them, caught unawares, were killed where they were found, at home, in the street, or in the temple. Others were bodily heaved up from where they were and taken and thrown at Sulla's feet. Others were dragged through the

38

streets and kicked to death, the spectators being too frightened to utter a word of protest at the horrors they witnessed. Others were expelled from Rome or had their property and belongings confiscated. Spies were abroad, looking everywhere for those who had fled the city, and killing any that they caught.

(Appian, *Civil Wars*, 1. 11)

Sulla then reorganized the constitution to put power effectively back into the hands of the upper classes. He re-established the original right of the senate to veto an act of any of the other assemblies, and virtually nullified the traditional influence of the tribunes of the people. He doubled the membership of the senate by admitting some 300 knights and selected Italian holders of office in outlying municipalities. He also made the holding of a quaestorship an automatic qualification for membership of the senate, and raised the number of quaestors to ten. This, together with the re-application of the statutory ten-year gap between holding the same office and the introduction of a new regulation that two years had to elapse between the holding of an office and election to the one above it, meant that there were now more junior state officials seeking fewer senior posts, and having to wait longer for them. As the competition grew, the ambitious were prepared to resort to unconstitutional means to achieve their aims.

Sulla's reforms of the legal system were less contentious. He established new courts to deal with specific offences, and crystallized the distinctions between civil and criminal law, though he removed the right of anyone except senior senators to adjudicate in lawsuits.

After three years of a reversion to what constituted an absolute monarchy, Sulla retired in 79 BC to his estate at Puteoli, and, like many politicians since, wrote his memoirs. He died not much more than a year later, of a thoroughly nasty dose of phthiriasis. It was the end of an era, even though technically the Roman republic had some fifty years still to run.

3

THE CAESARS

The twenty years that followed Sulla's death saw the rise of three men of particular ambition and power, and the flowering of the political and forensic skills of a fourth. Marcus Licinius Crassus (d. 53 BC) had prodigious wealth; Gnaeus Pompeius Magnus (106–48 BC), 'Pompey the Great', was a born military leader and organizer; Gaius Julius Caesar (102–44 BC) was both a military genius and an astute politician. Together they took advantage of Caesar's election as consul in 60 BC to form a triumvirate, which ruled unconstitutionally for several years. Marcus Tullius Cicero (106–43 BC) lived through these times and left to posterity many examples of his oratorical and prose styles in the form of speeches and letters. All four were stabbed to death within ten years of each other.

Cicero, like Marius, was born near Arpinum. He and his brothers were sent to Rome to complete their education, which was interrupted by military service in 89 BC. Cicero's first important speech in the courts was in defence of a man called Roscius, charged with murdering his father, the penalty for which under Roman law was to be tied up in a sack with a dog, a cock, a viper, and an ape, and then thrown into the nearest river. It was a brave case to take on, for the charge had been brought by one of Sulla's favourite freedmen, who had an interest in a conviction. Indeed, in Cicero's speech for the defence is the first recorded reference to the maxim *cui bono*: 'His honour Lucius Cassius [consul 127 BC, censor 125 BC], whom the Roman people regarded as the most responsible and wisest of judges, was in the habit of asking repeatedly during the course of a trial, "Who stood to gain?"' (*Pro Roscio Amerino*, XXX).

Roscius was acquitted, and Cicero prudently went abroad 'for reasons of health and study'. On his return to Rome after Sulla's death, he ascended the political ladder, helped by his oratory, which led the Sicilians to retain him as prosecutor in Rome of their former governor, Verres (d. 43 BC), a notorious embezzler and extortionist. Cicero's courtroom tactics, as well as his eloquence, were such that the defence counsel, up until then the leader of the Roman 'bar', threw up his brief while the evidence was still being called. Cicero was elected consul for 63 BC, when he distinguished himself by dealing firmly with a conspiracy against the state led by Lucius Sergius Catilina. Having, by means of a speech in the senate, shamed Catiline into leaving Rome, he arrested his fellow conspirators and had them summarily executed on the recommendation of the senate. Catiline was killed in battle the following year. The turning point in Cicero's career came in 61 BC, when he appeared in court, this time as a witness, and destroyed the alibi of one Publius Clodius (d. 52 BC), accused of attending in drag a 'ladies only' religious ceremony in honour of 'Bona Dea'. Clodius was not only powerful, but he was a toady of Caesar, who used Clodius in this instance as a means of driving Cicero into exile. For Cicero had refused to join the ruling triumvirate of Caesar, Crassus, and Pompey, and had gone even further and criticized its right to govern. Caesar only reluctantly agreed to Cicero's return in 57 BC.

Crassus had begun his trail to wealth and fame by buying cheap, from the state, the estates of those who had been proscribed by Sulla. He also had on call a team of 500 slaves who were skilled builders. He would wait for a fire in the city, which was never long in coming, as fire-risks were high, houses were crammed together, and there was then no fire service. At the first alarm, he rushed out and made a nominal offer not just for the burning house but for all the houses in the neighbourhood. In this way, and by rebuilding the damaged properties, he is said at one time or another to have owned most of Rome. He used much of his wealth to gain popular favour, both essential assets for an aspiring politician. As the supreme commander appointed by the senate in 72 BC against the slave revolt of Spartacus the gladiator, he is remembered for two acts. After his second-in-command had disobeyed orders and engaged the enemy with disastrous results, he revived the ancient punishment of decimation, dividing the 500 men he felt were most culpable for the actual defeat into fifty tens, and then choosing by lot one out of each ten to be publicly executed before the whole army. When, as praetor in 71 BC, he finally defeated Spartacus, he crucified the 6,000 survivors of the battle and left them to hang at regular intervals along the main road from Rome to Capua, where the rising had started.

Crassus and Pompey were consuls in 70 BC, and again in 55 BC, after which Crassus solicited for and obtained the governorship of the province of Syria, with its promise of rich pickings. There, in a misguided attempt to add military laurels to his wealth, he determined to resolve the problem of the Parthians, who, having settled in the region in about 250 BC, were now gradually making inroads into surrounding territories. Crassus was ignominiously defeated, and was murdered while trying to negotiate terms of surrender. It is said that his head was then cut off and molten gold poured into his mouth, as a symbol of his greed.

Pompey, the consular colleague of Crassus on two occasions, was first elected in 70 BC while under the statutory age-limit and without having held any government office. He had, however, already served the state well as a soldier, having raised his own army in support of Sulla and won famous victories over the party of Marius in Africa and the renegade Sertorius in Spain. His next command, in 67 BC, was an unusual one – to rid the Mediterranean of its infestation of pirates, who were making things intolerable for the ships, trade, and peoples of all the surrounding coasts. These pirates held important captives for ransom, while victims of lesser status, who hoped their Roman citizenship would give them protection, were treated to a bizarre charade. The pirates would profess awe and fear, and then fetch Roman clothes and footwear for them to wear, in order, so they said, that others would not make the same mistake. This done, the unfortunate prisoners were, one by one, hoisted out on to a ship's ladder and made to climb down, rung by rung, into the sea. Any who resisted were simply tossed overboard. The ceremony of 'walking the plank' is thus an ancient one.

The resources and powers put at Pompey's disposal were enormous, and included 250 ships, 100,000 marines, and 4,000 cavalry from Rome alone, which he reinforced with what was volunteered by other interested nations. He divided the Mediterranean and the Black Sea, with the adjacent coast-lands, into sectors, each the responsibility of a deputy with his

Figure 5 Life-size bust of Pompey: a first-century AD copy of a contemporary likeness. (*Ny Carlsberg Glyptotek, Copenhagen*)

own forces. By a concerted sweep against the pirates and their strongholds, he forced them out of business in three months, taking 20,000 prisoners, most of whom he spared and offered employment as farmers.

The following year Pompey was transferred to a more conventional command, against Mithridates, the king of Pontus who had been a sore trial to the Romans, and to everyone else, in Asia Minor for over twenty years. Pompey succeeded completely where others had failed, and in the process considerably enlarged the Roman empire. Unwilling at that time to assume sole power in Rome, but anxious to keep it within his sights, he threw in his lot with Crassus and Caesar, whose daughter Julia he married in 59 BC, as his fourth wife. Though it was no doubt originally intended as a marriage of political convenience such as he had contracted before with Sulla's stepdaughter, who was forced to divorce her husband by whom she was at the time pregnant, it seems to have been a successful partnership while it lasted. So much so that Julia's death in childbirth in 54 BC gives plausible substance to the account of the origins of the civil war given by the young literary prodigy, Lucan (AD 39–65), in his epic poem, *Pharsalia*:

> Julia alone, if granted by the fates a longer life, could have restrained her resentful husband, and her father, too; could have pushed aside their swords and joined the hands that held the weapons, just as the Sabine brides stood between their fathers and their men, who were then reconciled. Her death shattered family ties and released the enmity between the two. Ambition spurred them both. Pompey feared the exploits of his rival would obscure his own less recent triumphs; that the hammer of the pirates would take second place in people's esteem to the conqueror of Gaul. Caesar was driven by his craving for continuous activity and by a nature which would not let him give way. Caesar could not bear anyone to be his superior, nor Pompey to have an equal.
>
> *(Pharsalia,* I. 114–26)

What is equally probable is that Caesar, at the end of his campaign in Gaul, wanting a further consulship and command, and fearing prosecution for past irregularities if he did not get them, deliberately provoked the confrontation. He returned at the head of his army, had himself appointed temporary dictator, and pushed Pompey, his army, and his senatorial supporters out of Italy and to final defeat in 48 BC at Pharsalus in Greece. Pompey himself escaped, but was assassinated, before the eyes of his fifth wife, by officials of the Egyptian government, with whom he was seeking asylum, as he stepped ashore.

Caesar, in hot pursuit of Pompey, was then persuaded by Cleopatra (68–30 BC), joint ruler of Egypt with her brother, to stay a while as her personal guest. He accepted her invitation with such pleasure that a son, called Caesarion, was born to them the following year. In the meantime Caesar had been confirmed in his absence as dictator, an appointment which was regularly renewed thereafter. Thus began, with a few *interregna*, the rule of Rome by twelve men who successively held the name Caesar, by birth, by adoption, by descent through the female line, or by incorporating it into their official title. Gaius Suetonius Tranquillus (the historian Suetonius, AD 70–*c.* 140) wrote a racy and anecdotal account of them under the title 'Lives of the Caesars'.

JULIUS CAESAR

Gaius Julius Caesar: born on 12 July 100 BC in Rome, son of Gaius Caesar and Aurelia. Governor of Gaul 58–49 BC. Appointed dictator for ten years in 47 BC; for life, 14 February 44 BC. Married [1] Cornelia (one daughter, Julia); [2] Pompeia; [3] Calpurnia. Assassinated on 15 March 44 BC. Deified in 42 BC.

He was embarrassed by his baldness, which was a frequent subject of jokes on the part of his opponents; so much so that he used to comb his straggling locks forward from the back, and of all the honours heaped upon him by senate and people, the one he appreciated most was to be able to wear a laurel wreath at all times.

(Suetonius: *Julius Caesar,* XLV)

At the age of 30, arguably the most famous Roman of them all was regarded as a dandy who had squandered his wife's fortune (they married when he was 17) as well as his own. He was, however, a fine public speaker, which served him well when campaigning successfully for the offices of quaestor (he served in Spain); aedile (his extravagance in providing gladiatorial shows and renovating public buildings at his own expense to gain further popularity put him even deeper in debt); and praetor in 63 BC, when, according to Suetonius, baulked of his attempt to be appointed governor of Egypt, he resorted to 'massive bribery' in order to be elected *pontifex maximus.* His duties as praetor took him to Spain, where he discovered a talent as a military commander and amassed enough by way of booty and tribute to pay off his debts.

The formation of the ruling triumvirate with Crassus and Pompey was a mark also of Caesar's determination to push through genuine and innovative measures in the face of a senate which was suspicious of his motives, and to ensure that there was some continuity of progressive legislation after his year of office as consul was over. He then obtained for himself the governorship of Gaul for a period of five years, which was later extended for a second term. Gaul at that time comprised the subjugated region south of the Alps and to the east of the Apennines as far as the river Rubicon, together with a small portion of territory the other side of the Alps roughly corresponding to Provence and Languedoc. When Caesar had finished his series of brilliant but punitive campaigns, during which 2 million men, women, and children are said to have died, he was master of the whole region to the west of the Rhine, which he twice crossed to ensure that there would be no further trouble from the Germanic tribes. The size of the military operation was matched by its complexity. Even Lucius Annaeus Florus (*fl. c.* AD 130), who compiled his *Epitome of Roman History* in the form of a selective panegyric, underestimates Caesar's real achievement in his subjugation in 51 BC of Alesia, the fortified hill-city in which Vercingetorix, the Arvernian chief who most successfully opposed Rome, made his final stand.

> This mighty city, garrisoned by 80,000 troops, was defended by its walls, its fortress, and sheer river banks [on both sides]. Caesar invested it with an earth wall, a fence of stakes, and a moat, into which he diverted water from the river. His wall was topped with a massive parapet and had eighteen towers built into it. First he starved the inhabitants out. Then, when they dared to sally forth, he cut them down at the wall and the fence, and finally forced them to surrender.
>
> (*Epitome*, I. 46)

Florus fails to mention that at the same time Caesar had to cope with a Gaulish relief force of 250,000 infantry and 8,000 cavalry, whom he forced back and finally routed.

It was also in part a naval operation. In 55 and 54 BC Caesar mounted expeditions to Britain, which had up until then been unknown to the Roman world. From his own account of his final departure:

> After taking delivery of hostages, Caesar took his army back to the coast, where he found that the ships had been repaired. When he had refloated them, he decided, since he had so many prisoners and some ships had been lost in a storm, to make two trips. And it was a fact that with all those ships and so many crossings, neither in that or the previous year did any sink while carrying troops. But of the ships that were returned empty from the continent – those which had disembarked the men from the first sailing and the reserve fleet of sixty ships which he had given Labienus [his second-in-command] orders from Britain to build – few made the crossing safely and of the rest almost all had to turn back. Caesar waited some time for them in vain, and then, lest he

might be prevented from sailing altogether by the time of year, the equinox being imminent, he was forced to pack the troops more closely together on board. The sea went completely calm. He sailed at the beginning of the second watch, making land at dawn with the whole fleet intact.

(*Gallic War*, V. 23)

When Caesar left his province in 49 BC and crossed the Rubicon at the head of his troops, it was the signal that he came as an invader. After Pompey's hasty departure and ultimate defeat, and his own fruitful holiday in Egypt, Caesar returned to Rome with his army via Asia Minor, pausing at Zela to annihilate the forces of Pharnaces of Pontus (d. 47 BC), son of Mithridates. This was the occasion of his celebrated message to the senate, '*Veni, vidi, vici* (I came, I saw, I conquered)!' Opposition from the Pompeian faction, however, was only stamped out after two more campaigns, in Africa and Spain, culminating at the battle of Munda on 17 March 45 BC. In October of that year Caesar was back in Rome. Five months later he was dead, at the hands of a band of senatorial conspirators led by Marcus Junius Brutus (d. 42 BC) and Gaius Cassius Longinus (d. 42 BC), former Pompeians whom he had pardoned after the battle of Pharsalus. In the meantime he had established order, begun measures to reduce congestion in Rome and to drain large tracts of marshy land, given full voting rights to the inhabitants of his former province south of the Alps, revised the tax laws of Asia and Sicily, resettled many Romans in new homes in the Roman provinces, and reformed the calendar, which, with one slight adjustment, is the one in use today.

In Shakespeare's play *Julius Caesar*, the best lines, and the poetry, are given to Mark Antony's defence of Caesar's actions and his denial of any exercise of 'ambition' on Caesar's part, while Brutus, the leading conspirator in his murder, is left to justify himself in prose: 'As Caesar loved me, I weep for him; as he was fortunate, I rejoice at it; as he was valiant, I honour him; but, as he was ambitious, I slew him' (III. 2). The judgement of history is that Caesar's driving ambition and energy led him to try to make too many changes too quickly and without ensuring that there were workable substitutes for the traditions he was sweeping away. Further, the senate was concerned not so much

47

Figure 6 The Ides of March! Silver *denarius* issued by Brutus in 43/42 BC to celebrate his murder of Julius Caesar. It carries two daggers, a cap of liberty, and the date of the assassination, [E]ID. MAR. (×2)

with reverting to democracy, but with preserving rule by the aristocracy, and their positions in that rule. Later in the same scene in *Julius Caesar*, Mark Antony is made to say:

> You all did see that on the Lupercal,
> I thrice presented him a kingly crown,
> Which he did thrice refuse.
>
> (III. 2.101–3)

This is historical fact. Caesar's position was that of a king, but his refusal of the crown was for reasons of diplomacy, not modesty. In that the *imperium* that Caesar assumed gave him the position of sole ruler, he was in effect the first emperor of Rome. A literal translation of *imperium* would not be precisely 'command' or 'power', but something akin to both. The word *imperium* is related to *imperator*, which came to mean 'emperor' but was originally the title bestowed on a victorious military commander by his troops. Emperors got into the habit of collecting such a salutation each time a commander won a victory in their name: hence on coins of Domitian, for example, 'IMPERATOR XIIII' indicates that he had been acclaimed as victor in war fourteen times (see Figure 13).

The package of powers that Julius Caesar's successor assumed in 27 BC gave him the constitutional right to greater *imperium* than anyone else at the time. It is for this reason that the establishment of the rule of Rome by emperors is said to have begun then.

AUGUSTUS

Gaius Julius Caesar Octavianus: born on 23 September 63
BC in Rome, son of Gaius Octavius and Atia, niece of Julius
Caesar, who adopted him as his heir. Consul 43, 33, 31–23 BC.
Effectively became emperor in 27 BC, with extended civil powers
in 23 BC. Married [1] Claudia; [2] Scribonia (one daughter,
Julia); [3] Livia Drusilla, mother of Tiberius. Died at Nola, 19
August AD 14. Deified on 17 September AD 14.

> He was of distinguished and extremely handsome appearance for
> the whole of his life, though for himself he did not care what he
> looked like. He would have several barbers working feverishly on
> him simultaneously, and while he was being shaved or having his
> hair clipped (it was all one to him) he read or even carried on with
> his writing. . . . He had bad teeth, small and widely set apart; his
> hair was fair and wavy; his eyebrows met in the middle of his
> forehead; his ears were of average size; his nose jutted out at the
> top and then bent downwards.
>
> (Suetonius: *Augustus*, LXXIX)

The owner of this indubitably Roman nose was in Apollonia in
Epirus, pursuing his military studies, when he heard of his great-
uncle's murder, and that in his will Caesar had named him not
only his son by adoption, but also his principal heir. In was late
April when he got back to Rome, by which time Marcus
Antonius (c. 83–30 BC) – Mark Antony – and Marcus Aemilius
Lepidus (d. 13 BC), who had been Caesar's chief assistants, had
assumed control of the state, and of Caesar's personal fortune,
and Brutus and the other conspirators had, at the prompting of
Cicero, been granted an amnesty by the senate. A confused
series of battles and comings and goings resulted in Octavian
(as he was then styled) being elected consul, at the age of 19, and
forcing through a motion to the effect that he, Antony, and
Lepidus should formally be recognized as the ruling triumvirate
for five years. Their first act was to revive the fearful Sullan
policy of proscription.

> As soon as they were on their own, the three drew up a list of
> those who were to die. They proscribed, both then and later,
> those of whom they were suspicious because of their ability,
> as well as their personal enemies, trading with each other for
> the lives of their own relations and friends. They decreed

death and confiscation of property for about 300 senators and 2,000 knights, among them their own brothers and uncles, as well as senior officers serving under them who had had cause to offend them or their own colleagues. As they left the conference table for Rome they decided to postpone most of the killings, but as a warning secretly to send out assassins to execute twelve, or some say seventeen, of the most important victims, including Cicero.

(Appian, *Civil Wars*, IV. 2)

Cicero was too ill to escape his murderers, but was bundled into a litter by his slaves. He was tracked down and killed by a sword-cut to the neck. His head and hands were cut off and sent to Rome where, on the orders of Antony, they were nailed up in the forum.

While the triumvirate formally remained in power beyond its statutory term, the twelve years until 31 BC were almost entirely taken up with wars between its members, and against other fellow Romans. Brutus and Cassius were defeated in two battles at Philippi in Macedonia in 42 BC, and committed suicide. Sextus Pompey (son of Pompey the Great by his third wife), having obtained a large fleet and taken possession of Sicily, was finally murdered by his own troops in 35 BC. Antony's long-standing affair with Caesar's former mistress, Cleopatra, and his preference for her company and Alexandria over that of his wife and Rome, culminated in Octavian's defeat of the Egyptian fleet at the battle of Actium in 31 BC.

The queen was the first to take flight, the golden stern and purple sails of her galley disappearing into the open sea. Antony soon followed, with Octavian surging in his wake. . . . Antony was the first to commit suicide, by the sword. Cleopatra threw herself at Octavian's feet, and tried her best to attract his gaze: in vain, for his self-control was impervious to her beauty. It was not her life she was after, for that had already been granted, but a portion of her kingdom. When she realized this was hopeless and that she had been earmarked to feature in Octavian's triumph in Rome, she took advantage of her guard's carelessness to get herself into the mausoleum, as the royal tomb is called. Once there, she put on the royal robes which she was accustomed to wear, and lay down in a richly perfumed coffin beside her Antony.

50

Then she applied poisonous snakes to her veins and slipped into death as though into a sleep.

(Florus, *Epitome*, II. 21)

With Lepidus now a back number and Caesarion murdered, Octavian was in charge of the Roman world. He needed to assemble his powers into an acceptable constitutional form, avoiding any suggestion of a return to a monarchy or even to a dictatorship, which had caused so much trouble in the past. He achieved this gradually over a number of years, and in a manner which did not appear to undermine the authority of the senate, at least as a consultative body. While continuing to hold successive consulates, in 27 BC he formally resigned all the special powers he had been granted, but accepted in return for ten years the strategic provinces of Cilicia, Cyprus, Gaul, Spain, and Syria, for which troops were required, together with his confirmation as divine successor to the pharaohs in Egypt. (His own account of the process was incorporated into one of the statements engraved on bronze tablets at the entrance to the family mausoleum which he built: 'During my sixth and seventh consulates [28 and 27 BC], when I had put down the civil wars and was universally acknowledged to be in complete control, I transferred the management of affairs of state to the senate and the Roman people' (*Res Gestae Divi Augusti*, 34).) In addition, he renounced the name of Octavian in favour of the more dignified Augustus. In 23 BC, because of illness, he gave up his apparent claim to hold the office of consul for life. This was diplomatically a sound move, as it opened up to others an additional chance of honour if not much responsibility; especially as in its place he was granted the privileges of a tribune of the people, with powers to apply a veto at will and to take matters direct to the popular assemblies.

That particular illness proved to be only a minor set-back in a reign that lasted over forty years and gave to the western world the term 'Augustan' to denote an age of glittering literary achievement. Though the boundaries of the Roman empire had not yet reached their widest extent, Augustus consolidated them by strengthening the army and removing it from Italy to patrol the provinces. He remodelled the civil service and largely rebuilt parts of Rome itself, appointing 3,500 firemen under a chief fire officer to guard against conflagration.

Augustus died in the family house at Nola in Campania, at the age of 76. He was married three times, but his only child was a daughter by his second wife. He had, however, taken the precaution, after several attempts to do so had been aborted by deaths, of nominating a successor, his stepson Tiberius, to whom the previous year he had given a form of 'power of attorney' over affairs of state.

TIBERIUS

Tiberius Claudius Nero Caesar: born on 16 November 42 BC, son of Tiberius Claudius Nero (d. 33 BC) and Livia Drusilla (*c.* 58 BC–AD 29), who married Augustus in 39 BC. Became emperor in AD 14. Married [1] Vipsania (one son, Drusus 13 BC–AD 23); [2] Julia, daughter of Augustus. Died at Misenum, 16 March AD 37.

> He was a large, strong man of above average height, with broad shoulders and chest, and well-proportioned all the way from head to toe. He was left-handed, and his joints were so strong that he could bore through an apple with one finger, and break open a boy's or even a teenager's head with a mere rap of the knuckle. He wore his white hair long at the back, covering his neck, a family habit, apparently. He had a handsome face, which would, however, suddenly erupt into a fierce rash.
>
> (Suetonius, *Tiberius*, LXVIII)

Though Tiberius had been groomed by Augustus as his successor, he was actually fourth choice after Agrippa, husband of Augustus's only daughter Julia, and their sons, Gaius and Lucius, all three of whom died in the lifetime of Augustus. Thus to an already diffident nature was added a sense of inferiority. On Agrippa's death, Augustus compelled Tiberius to divorce his wife Vipsania and become Julia's third husband. Five years later, in 6 BC, in spite of his recent appointment to a five-year term as the equivalent of chief tribune of the people, a highly influential function up until then performed by Augustus himself, Tiberius asked for and was granted leave of absence, and retired to Rhodes. Of the reasons which have been suggested for this voluntary exile at such a critical point in his career, the behaviour of Julia seems not the least unlikely. Certainly, by the time he returned in AD 2, she had been banished by her father for adultery. In AD 4, Tiberius, now

52

adopted son of Augustus, was sent to command the imperial armies, all of them based outside Italy. From then until Augustus's death, which happened while he was travelling, he hardly had occasion to visit Rome.

Tiberius was summoned back not by the senate, but by his elderly mother, Livia, widow of Augustus. The circumstances of her marriage were bizarre, whatever interpretation is put on them. It is said that her first husband was forced to divorce her, and she married Augustus when she was six months pregnant with Tiberius's younger brother, Drusus; Augustus having divorced his own second wife, Scribonia, according to him because he was 'sick of her perpetual bitching' (Suetonius, *Augustus*, LXII), on the very day she gave birth to their only child. Livia had been only 15 when Tiberius was born: now approaching or in her seventies, she was a matriarch and she wanted a share in ruling the country, too. Tiberius would have none of that, but in order to secure his position, he had Agrippa junior, the last surviving grandson of Augustus, murdered, though some said this was organized by Livia without his knowledge.

There followed several years of intrigue and counter-intrigue, as candidates to succeed Tiberius (and their wives or mothers on their behalf) jockeyed for position or were jockeyed completely out of the way, as happened to Drusus, the emperor's only son. Tiberius probably had no part in any of this, but merely to sense what was going on unsettled him, and further contributed to his indecision in matters of government. Finally, in AD 26, he had had enough. Because he had probably always been happiest when away from Rome, he simply upped and departed to his holiday mansion on the isle of Capri, never to return to the city. He left administration in the hands of Lucius Aelius Sejanus (d. AD 31), praetorian prefect (commander of the imperial guard), who was, in his own mind at least, a contender for the post of emperor when it next fell vacant, and was conspiring against Tiberius while removing people in his own path. Tiberius, however, when moved to do so, could still exercise power even from a distance, and wrote a letter to the senate expressing his suspicions. Sejanus was executed, and his corpse dragged through the streets and then thrown into the Tiber. His family and many of his cronies suffered the same fate. The treatment of his children casts a chilling sidelight on the logic of the Roman penal system:

> Though the fury of the people was quietening down and many had been pacified by the earlier executions, it was then decided to attend to the two surviving children of Sejanus. They were therefore taken to jail, the boy realizing what was in store for them, the girl so innocent that she kept asking what she had done, crying that she would do nothing wrong again and that surely a gentle spanking would be enough this time. The archivists of the time record that because there was no legal precedent for the execution of a virgin, the hangman had intercourse with her beside the noose. The pair were then strangled and their bodies, young as they were, thrown on the steps by the Capitol.
>
> (Tacitus, *Annals*, VI. 5)

Tacitus (*c.* AD 55–*c.* 117) was only one of the Roman historians who suggested that Tiberius's retirement home was what might be termed a palace of sexual varieties, but he does add that Tiberius left for it 'with only a few companions: a former consul [and] . . . a Roman knight of the higher rank . . . the rest being intellectuals, mainly Greek, whose conversation he enjoyed' (*Annals*, IV. 58). Tiberius's last years were still fraught with morbid mistrust, reports of flagrant and not-quite-so-flagrant family adulteries, and a continual narrowing down, by natural and unnatural death, of candidates for the succession. Whether Tiberius, who was then 75, died naturally or was murdered, is uncertain, but by then the field had been reduced to two: his own grandson, Tiberius Gemellus (*c.* AD 20–37), who was, however, suspected by many, including Tiberius, to have been an outcome of his mother's affair with Sejanus; and his last surviving great-nephew, Gaius Caesar, now 24, nicknamed Caligula ('Bootsie') after the miniature army boots he used to wear as a child. With typical vacillation to the last, Tiberius named them joint heirs.

CALIGULA

Gaius Caesar: born in AD 12, son of Germanicus Caesar (15 BC–AD 19), nephew of Tiberius, and Agrippina (14 BC–AD 33), granddaughter of Augustus. Became emperor in AD 37. Married

54

[1] Junia Claudilla; [2] Livia Orestilla; [3] Lollia Paulina; [4] Caesonia (one daughter, Julia). Assassinated on 24 January AD 41.

> He was very tall, with an enormous body supported on spindly legs, a thin neck, and an extremely pallid complexion. His eyes and temples were sunken, and his forehead broad and glowering. His hair was thin and he was bald on top, though he had a hairy body. For that reason it was a crime punishable by death to look down on him from above as he passed by, or for any reason whatsoever to mention a goat in his presence. He was by nature ugly, but he made himself even more so by practising gruesome faces in a mirror.
>
> (Suetonius, *Caligula*, I)

The question as to who would succeed Tiberius was resolved easily enough. Naevius Cordus Sutorius Macro (d. AD 38), a former chief of the fire service in Rome and now commander of the imperial guard in succession to Sejanus, had met Caligula

Figure 7　Caligula: a chilling study of weakness and cruelty. (*Ny Carlsberg Glyptotek, Copenhagen*)

on Capri, and they got on well together. When he proposed Caligula's name to the senate as emperor, there was no objection. At first, it seemed that the choice was correct, for Caligula was everything a young and charismatic ruler should be – generous to the public (and to the imperial guard), genuinely interested, though inexperienced, in matters of government, sensible, witty, and just. He recalled many political exiles and dropped the charges against them, and banished all male prostitutes. He formally adopted his cousin, Tiberius Gemellus, and appointed his uncle Claudius (his dead father's younger brother) to his first public office as consul. Then he fell ill. When he recovered, the citizens of Rome found they were living in a nightmare.

According to Suetonius, Caligula had since childhood suffered from epilepsy, known in Roman times as the 'parliamentary disease', since it was regarded as an especially bad omen if anyone had a fit while public business was being conducted – Caligula's very distant cousin, Julius Caesar, also suffered occasional attacks. This, or some other cause, violently affected his mental state, and he became totally irrational, with delusions not only of grandeur but also of divinity. He put Tiberius Gemellus and Macro to death without trial. To have an altar built to himself was one thing: it was quite another to propose that statues of himself be erected in synagogues. His extravagance knew no bounds, and he introduced heavy taxation to help balance his personal expenditure. In such an atmosphere, executions and displays of sheer bloodlust were commonplace, and conspiracies and plots proliferated. Finally the inevitable happened: one of the plots succeeded. He was assassinated by members of his imperial guard. Caligula had been emperor for less than four years. He had four wives, three of them during his imperial reign – the last, Caesonia, and their daughter Julia were murdered at the same time as him – and he was said to have committed incest with each of his three sisters in turn.

CLAUDIUS

Tiberius Claudius Drusus Nero Germanicus Caesar: born on 1 August 10 BC at Lugdunum, Gaul, son of Nero Claudius Drusus (38–9 BC), brother of Tiberius, and Antonia (36 BC–AD 37), daughter of Mark Antony. Became emperor in AD

Figure 8   Claudius as the god Jupiter: a larger than life-size marble statue of about AD 55. There is no doubt about his intelligence; it has been suggested that the garb and pose represent a deliberate attempt at mockery on the part of the artist. (*Deutsches Archaeologisches Institut, Rome*)

41. Married [1] Plautia Urgulanilla (one son, Drusus, d. *c.* AD 26, and one daughter, Claudia); [2] Aelia Paetina (one daughter, Antonia); [3] Valeria Messalina (one son, Tiberius Claudius Britannicus, AD 41–55, and one daughter, Octavia, d. AD 62); [4] Agrippina. Died on 12 October AD 54. Deified in AD 54.

He was not short of either authority or dignity when he was standing up or sitting down, still less so when he reclined: he was tall but not lanky, and good-looking, with a fine crop of white hair and a well-set neck. But his knees were so weak that he staggered as he walked, and his habits were embarrassing whether he was indulging in domestic or business affairs. He had an indecent laugh, and when he was annoyed he foamed disgustingly at the mouth and his nose ran. He stammered, and his head twitched the whole time, but faster when he was actually engaged in the slightest activity. He was always ill, until he became emperor. Then his health improved marvellously, except for attacks of stomach-ache, which he said even made him think of suicide.

(Suetonius, *Claudius*, XXX, XXXI)

After the assassination of Caligula, members of the imperial guard who were systematically sacking the palace came across his uncle Claudius cowering behind a curtain. Possibly they saw him as a useful hostage in the event of retribution, for, instead of killing him, they pushed him into a litter and carried him off to their camp. There he was made an offer: to be the imperial guard's nominee as emperor. Obviously feeling that to be emperor was a fate not quite as bad as immediate death, Claudius cemented the deal by promising a special bonus in return for their support, thus creating a precedent which future aspirants had to follow. In the absence of any other obvious candidate, the senate confirmed the choice of the imperial guard. Claudius was then 50. He was a scholar – the author of historical works in both Latin and Greek, though none has survived, and the inventor of three new letters of the alphabet, which have come down to us in inscriptions – but without experience of administration, let alone of government.

In history and in the accounts of ancient historians, Claudius comes across as a positive mishmash of conflicting characteristics: absent-minded, hesitant, muddled, determined, cruel (by proxy), intuitive, wise, and dominated by his wife and his personal staff of freedmen. He was probably all of these. If his choice of women was disastrous, there are countless instances of this particular failing on the part of prominent public figures. And he may, with sound reasoning, have preferred the advice of educated and trained executives from abroad to that of potentially suspect aristocratic senators, even if some of those executives *did* use their influence to their own financial advantage. It was a thoroughly sound if not glittering reign, which lasted almost fourteen years: even if it did end in violence, at least it was by poison at the hands of his wife, not by the sword of a political assassin.

Claudius revived the office of censor, which had fallen into disuse, and took on the job himself, introducing into the senate as new members several chiefs from Gaul. With the help of his personal staff, he reorganized and rationalized the financial affairs of the state and empire, setting aside a separate fund for the emperor's private household expenses. Almost all grain had to be imported, mainly from Africa and Egypt. To encourage potential importers and to build up stocks against winter months and times of famine, Claudius offered to insure them against losses on the open sea, an unusual provision in ancient times. To make unloading easier and to relieve congestion in the river Tiber, he carried out a scheme originally proposed by Julius Caesar, and constructed the new port of Ostia on the coast. Unfortunately it was built to the north of the Tiber mouth, with a channel connecting the two, which meant that the prevailing current from the sea deposited in the harbour accumulations of silt brought down by the river.

Claudius's most far-reaching initiative led to the first successful full-scale invasion of Britain, after a reconnaissance by the expedition's leader, Aulus Plautius. Rome could no longer pretend that Britain did not exist, and a potentially hostile and possibly united nation just beyond the fringe of the existing empire presented a threat which could not be ignored. Besides, Claudius, for so long the butt of his family, wanted a piece of military glory, and here was a chance to get it. The force which sailed in AD 43 was a formidable one, even by Roman standards. Whether Plautius had instructions to call on Claudius if he got into difficulties or simply to invite him over to preside at the kill is not clear. He did get into difficulties, however. The only surviving account of the campaign is by Dio Cassius (*c.* AD

Figure 9 Gold *aureus* (AD 46/7) of Claudius celebrating his British victory. On the reverse is a triumphal arch and the words DE BRITANN. (×2)

155–235), of Nicaea, governor of Africa and then Dalmatia, who wrote in Greek.

Shortly afterwards Togodumnus [son of the British king Cunobellinus – Cymbeline – who died between AD 40 and 43] was killed, but the Britons, so far from giving up, were all the more united now in a determination to avenge his death. Plautius, unwilling to advance any farther, consolidated the territory he had gained and sent for Claudius. His orders were to do this if he met any resistance, and extensive preparations for just such an eventuality, including the mobilization of an elephant corps, had already been made. When he received the message, Claudius handed over the administration of affairs at home and abroad, including military operations, to his consular colleague Lucius Vitellius (having fixed for both of them a further full six months in office), and then himself took the field. He went by river to Ostia, and then sailed along the coast to Massilia [Marseilles]. From there, travelling overland and by river transport, he reached the sea and crossed to Britain, where he met up with his troops, who were encamped by the river Thames.

Assuming command, he crossed the river, engaged the barbarians, who had rallied together at his approach, defeated them, and took Camelodunum [Colchester], Cunobellinus's capital. Then he put down many other tribes, defeating them or accepting their surrender, and was hailed as *imperator* numerous times, which was against the rules, for no one could receive this honour more than once in the same campaign. He confiscated the tribes' weapons, which he handed over to Plautius with orders to subdue the rest. He then returned to Rome, sending news of his victory ahead with his sons-in-law, Magnus and Silanus. When the senate heard about his achievement, it granted him the title of Britannicus and authorized him to celebrate a triumph.

(Roman History, LX. 21)

Claudius was in Britain just sixteen days. Plautius followed up the advantage gained, and was from AD 44 to 47 governor of this newest province in the Roman empire. When Caratacus (brother of Togodumnus) was finally captured and brought to Rome in chains, Claudius pardoned him and his family.

Claudius was married four times; in spite of his physical disadvantages he was more successful in fathering progeny than any of his imperial predecessors, if rather less lucky in love. At his succession, he was on his third wife, Messalina, who three weeks later presented him with a son (afterwards known as Britannicus, the title having been conferred on him by a grateful, or perhaps astonished, senate at the same time as on his father). Eventually Messalina was discovered too many times *in flagrante delicto,* and in AD 48, aged about 24, she was duly disposed of by tried Roman methods. Speculation was rife as to who would be the next imperial consort. It turned out to be Agrippina (AD 15–59), Caligula's sister and Claudius's own niece, to marry whom he had first to have a law enacted permitting such unions. By a former marriage Agrippina had a teenage son, later known as Nero. She persuaded Claudius to adopt him formally, and to give Nero his daughter Octavia in marriage. Then she poisoned him.

NERO

Nero Claudius Caesar Drusus Germanicus: born Lucius Domitius Ahenobarbus at Antium in AD 37, son of Gnaeus Domitius Ahenobarbus, consul in AD 32, and Agrippina, sister of Caligula, who then married Crispus Passienus and, later, in AD 49, her uncle Claudius. Became emperor in AD 54. Married [1]

Figure 10 Gold *aureus* issued in AD 54, the first year of Nero's reign, showing the new emperor and his mother, Agrippina, who had contrived his appointment. He later had her murdered! (×2)

Octavia; [2] Poppaea Sabina (one daughter, Claudia Augusta, who died in infancy); [3] Statilia Messalina. Committed suicide in AD 68.

> He was of average height, fair-haired, with features that were pretty rather than handsome, weak blue eyes, a fat neck, a pot belly, skinny legs, and a body which smelt and was covered with spots. . . . He was so insensitive about his appearance that he used to wear his hair in rows of curls, and when he was on his Greek trip he let it grow down his back. He usually appeared in public in a dressing-gown without a belt, a scarf round his neck, and no shoes.
>
> (Suetonius, *Nero*, LI)

Nero was artistic, sporting, brutal, weak, sensual, erratic, extravagant, sadistic, bisexual – and latterly almost certainly deranged. He was 16 when his mother secured for him the office of emperor, by engineering his being presented to the troops as their candidate and by promising what was now the customary bonus. Shortly afterwards the only other possible contender, Claudius's son Britannicus, was removed, almost certainly by poison. During the early years of his reign, however, Nero was kept in hand by his tutor, the distinguished philosopher and writer, Lucius Annaeus Seneca, now in his early sixties, and Africanus Burrus, praetorian prefect, though exceptionally persuasive tactics had to be employed to get the emperor to withdraw, and forget, a proposal to abolish all taxation. Nero's excesses of behaviour were hushed up, if not entirely restrained, and between the three of them they managed also to avert attempts by Agrippina to exert imperial influence. The turning point came largely through Nero's inherent lust and lack of self-control, for he took, as his (not uncomplaisant) mistress, Poppaea, wife of his partner in frequent debaucheries, Marcus Salvius Otho, five years his senior, whom in AD 58 he dispatched to be governor of Lusitania. Agrippina, presumably seeing this as an opportunity to assert herself, sided with Nero's wife, Octavia. Nero retaliated, according to Suetonius, with a grotesque and abortive series of attempts on his mother's life, including three by poison and one by engineering – the ceiling above her bed was geared to collapse while she was asleep. Finally (and here the accounts of Suetonius and Tacitus agree) he had a collapsible boat constructed, which was meant to deposit her in the Bay of Naples. It did, but she swam ashore. Nero sent a man to her house to use more conventional means. She was clubbed and stabbed to death.

That happened in AD 59. Nero celebrated by redoubling his outbreaks of excessive licentiousness and by creating two new festivals of chariot-racing, athletics, and musical contests, which gave him further opportunities to demonstrate in public his talent for singing while accompanying himself on the lyre. No one was allowed to leave the auditorium while he was performing, for whatever reason. Suetonius writes of women giving birth during a Nero recital, and of men who pretended to die and were carried out as if to burial.

Burrus died in AD 62. Soon after that Seneca retired, whereupon Nero became totally subject to corrupt and evil advisers, indulging to the exclusion of everything else his passions for sport, music, preposterous parties, at which he and his guests publicly performed sexual acts of unimaginable ingenuity, and murder. Having divorced Octavia in AD 62 and then had her executed on a trumped-up charge of adultery, he married Poppaea, now divorced, and then killed her too – Suetonius says he kicked her to death when she complained at his coming home late from the races. In AD 65 there was a genuine conspiracy to assassinate him; when it was discovered there was terrible retribution in which Seneca and his nephew, the poet Lucan, died. There was never anything even resembling a trial: people whom Nero suspected or disliked or who merely aroused the jealousy of his advisers were sent a note ordering them to commit suicide. Gaius Petronius, man of letters and former 'director of imperial pleasures', died in this manner in AD 66. So did countless senators, noblemen, and generals, including in AD 67 Gnaeus Domitius Corbulo, hero of the Armenian wars and supreme commander in the Euphrates region.

In AD 64 fire had ravaged Rome for six days on end. According to Tacitus, who was about 9 years old at the time, of the fourteen districts of the city, 'four were undamaged, three were utterly destroyed, and in the other seven there remained only a few mangled and half-burnt traces of houses' (*Annals*, XV. 40). This is the famous occasion on which Nero is said to have 'fiddled while Rome burned', a phrase which in that form seems first to have emerged in the seventeenth century. Suetonius has him singing from a tower overlooking the conflagration. Dio Cassius records that he 'climbed on to the palace roof, from which there was the best overall view of the greater part of the fire and, assuming the garb of a lyre player, sang "The Capture of Troy"' (*Roman History*, LX. 18). Tacitus has a similar story: 'At the very time that Rome burned, he mounted his private stage and, reflecting present disasters in ancient calamities, sang about the destruction of Troy' (*Annals*, XV. 39), but he is careful to qualify it as *rumor*, 'an unauthenticated report'. The mere report, however, made people suspicious of the genuine relief measures which Nero immediately initiated. Nor was faith in his motives increased when he used a vast tract of ground razed by the fire between the Palatine and Esquiline hills on which to build his 'Golden Palace', a vast luxury complex (with two different kinds of running water) set in rambling pleasure gardens, specially designed for his amusements. It did not matter that he had residential areas elsewhere in the city rebuilt at his own expense to a proper grid pattern, with broad streets and open spaces. People said that they missed the cool shade of the original alleys and the towering, ramshackle tenements. Rumours of arson surfaced again, and Nero, looking around for scapegoats, found them in the members of the latest religious sect, Christianity, many of whom were rounded up and torn to death by dogs or crucified as a public spectacle. The killings went on throughout the day and into the night, when more victims were burned to death to serve as street lighting, while Nero mingled with the crowds, driving his personal chariot.

Finally the tide of organized revolt gathered pace. In AD 68 one of the governors in Gaul, Gaius Julius Vindex, himself Gallic-born, withdrew his oath of allegiance to the emperor and encouraged the governor of northern and eastern Spain, Galba, a hardened veteran of 71, to do the same. Vindex's troops were suppressed by legions who marched in from Germany, and Vindex committed suicide. Galba, having informed the senate that he was available, if required, to head a government, waited, and presumably sweated. The senate, obviously relieved that someone else was prepared to take personal responsibility, not only declared Nero a public enemy, but sentenced him to death by flogging. Nero thought of flight, dithered, and then killed himself with the help of his secretary.

GALBA

Servius Sulpicius Galba: born on 24 December 3 BC near Tarracina. Governor of Hispania Tarraconensis AD 61–8. Became emperor in AD 68. Married Lepida (two sons); all three died early in his career. Assassinated on 15 January AD 69.

> He was of medium height, almost completely bald, blue-eyed, hook-nosed, and with feet and hands so crippled by arthritis that he could not wear shoes, or hold a book, let alone unroll it. His left side had grown outwards and hung down so far that it could only be held in with difficulty by a truss.
>
> (Suetonius, *Galba*, XXI)

Galba, who was the direct and sole surviving descendant of an old republican family, had been consul before being appointed commander of the army of Upper Germany, after which he went into retirement until being called back by Nero to become governor in Spain. He was old, a disciplinarian whose methods owed much to cruelty, and notoriously mean. His accession was notable on two counts. It marked the end of what is known as the Julio-Claudian dynasty – he assumed the name of Caesar when Nero's death was reported to him – and it proved that it was feasible for an emperor to emerge from, and be appointed, outside Rome itself. Nero died in the summer of AD 68; it was October before Galba arrived in the city, having in the meantime organized from a distance the murder of two other regional commanders-in-chief who had been slow to get their troops to swear allegiance to him as emperor. He then committed the solecism of refusing to pay the traditional bonus, which the imperial guard had been promised on his behalf.

Worse followed. On 2 January AD 69, the legions in Germany proclaimed as emperor their commanding officer, Aulus Vitellius, to whom the troops in Upper Germany also promised their support. Galba tried to stem the threat of civil war by naming a young man of noble republican birth, Marcius Piso Licinianus, as joint ruler and his successor. It was a disastrous choice, as Piso had neither qualifications nor personal distinction, and the appointment offended Otho, the former husband of Nero's Poppaea, now back in Rome after his ten-year stint in Lusitania. Otho immediately turned attention on himself by the simple and, by now, time-honoured ploy of bribing the imperial guard to support his cause. On 15 January, they swore their allegiance, marched into the city, and hacked Galba and Piso to death.

OTHO

Marcus Salvius Otho: born on 28 April AD 32. Governor of Lusitania AD 58–68. Became emperor on 15 January AD 69. Married Poppaea Sabina, future wife of Nero. Committed suicide on 14 April AD 69.

> He was quite small, with bow legs, and feet that stuck out at each side. He was almost as fastidious as a woman. His body was plucked and because his hair was so thin, he wore a wig, so well-made and closely fitting that no one suspected.
>
> (Suetonius, *Otho*, XII)

Otho's claims to a niche in history are few. It seems, however, that he performed creditably as governor of the province of Lusitania, to which Nero had sent him to get him out of the way. As emperor, his most immediate task was to overcome the threat of the other nominee, Vitellius, and this meant civil war. The armies of Upper and Lower Germany advanced into northern Italy, each by a different route across the Alps. Otho charged boldly out to meet them, crossed the Po, and was outflanked. His army surrendered and he committed suicide. He had been emperor for just three months.

VITELLIUS

Aulus Vitellius: born on 24 September AD 15. Became emperor in AD 69. Married [1] Petronia (one son); [2] Galeria Fundana (one son, one daughter). Assassinated on 24 December AD 69.

> He used to have three, or four, heavy meals a day: at least a full breakfast, lunch, and dinner, and a convivial drinks' party, for each of which he had himself invited to a different house, at a cost to his host of never less than 400,000 sesterces a time. He was easily able to consume the lot by indulging in frequent bouts of self-induced vomiting. . . . He was enormously tall, with a face usually purple with drink, a vast belly, and one thigh permanently damaged by a blow from a chariot, sustained while he was acting as Caligula's co-driver in a race.
>
> (Suetonius, *Vitellius*, XIII, XVII)

Vitellius, son of a former consul, was a man of some learning but little military skill or experience – his appointment, by Galba, to his command in Lower Germany had taken most people by surprise. In mid-July AD 69, he reached Rome and was officially recognized as emperor. He immediately celebrated with bouts of extravagant entertaining and betting on the races, and was sufficiently out of touch with public feeling that, after assuming the office also of *pontifex maximus*, he made a pronouncement about worship on a day which was traditionally regarded as unlucky. Even before this, on 1 July, the forces in the eastern Mediterranean had repudiated him and sworn their allegiance to Titus Flavius Vespasianus, commander in Palestine. The legions of the Danube, who had originally supported Otho, did likewise, and, while Vespasian waited in the wings, they marched into Italy without waiting for support. They met, and defeated, the imperial army near Cremona, and then made a dash for Rome, which capitulated. Vitellius was hunted down, driven out into the streets with his hands tied behind his back, and tortured to death. The date was 24 December AD 69. Within one year three successive emperors of Rome had died violently, and now a fourth was acclaimed.

Figure 11 A contemporary likeness of Vespasian: even the loss of the nose cannot detract from the impression of a tough but inherently kindly man. (*Ny Carlsberg Glyptotek, Copenhagen*)

VESPASIAN

Titus Flavius Sabinus Vespasianus: born on 17 November AD 9 at Reate. Served in Thrace, Crete, Cyrene, Germany, Britain, and Africa. Military commander in Palestine AD 66–9. Became emperor in AD 69. Married Flavia Domitilla, who died *c.* AD 65 (two sons, Titus and Domitian, and one daughter, Domitilla). Died at Reate on 24 June AD 79. Deified in AD 79.

This was his usual daily routine while emperor. He rose early, even while it was still dark. Then, after reading his letters and abstracts of official reports, he let in his friends, and while they chatted to him put on his shoes himself and got dressed. When he had dealt with any business that cropped up, he would find time for a drive and then a lie down with a concubine, of whom he had several to take the place of his dead mistress, Caenis. After that he had a bath and then went through to dinner; it is said that he was at his most approachable and amenable at that time, so his household were eager to seize the opportunity of asking him something then.

(Suetonius, *Vespasian*, XXI)

If a temporary return to a dynastic succession can be said in itself to represent a constitutional change for the better, then sanity and internal peace were for a time restored with the appointment of Vespasian. He was almost 61 when he arrived back in Rome in October AD 70, but he was still fit and active, and he had two sons, Titus and Domitian, aged 29 and 19 respectively. Titus was left in Palestine to continue the campaign to reduce the Jewish population to submission. This he did with undoubted, if misguided, skill and panache, taking Jerusalem in September AD 70. On his return to Rome in AD 71, Vespasian formally made him his associate in government, granting him too the title of Caesar, and appointed him commander of the imperial guard, a sound move in the light of the success that body had had in altering the balance of power.

Vespasian was of middle-class upbringing. His mother's father had been a senior army officer, and one of her brothers had reached the rank of praetor and had sat in the senate. He was a professional soldier who as legionary commander had served with considerable distinction during the first assault by Aulus Plautius on Britain, and had been responsible for taking the Isle of Wight. This success led to Vespasian's election as consul for AD 51, and later to his appointment as governor of Africa, before being sent by Nero to conduct the war against the Jews. More significantly for the present predicament of Rome, he had neither the time nor the liking for the extravagant life, and he was a brilliant and tireless administrator, with a gift, so often lacking in his predecessors, of picking the right man for a job. In AD 74 he had recognized the potential of Gnaeus Julius Agricola (AD 40–93), later the father-in-law of Tacitus:

When Agricola returned from the command of his legion [in Britain], the divine Vespasian made him a member of the patrician class and appointed him governor of Aquitania, a post of great distinction from the point of view both of the status of the job and the promise it offered of a consulate, for which Vespasian had marked him out.

(Tacitus, *Agricola*, IX)

Figure 12   The remains of the man-made ramp, rising 140 metres up to the rock-fortress of Masada, overlooking the Dead Sea. It testifies to Roman tenacity and engineering skill, and to the desperate determination of the Jewish community of 960 men, women, and children, who in AD 72–3 defied all attempts at capture. Archaeological evidence discovered in 1963–5 largely confirms the account of Josephus in his history of the Jewish wars, written at the command of Vespasian. All materials, as well as provisions and water, had to be carried over the vast stretch of desert plateau. The defenders finally committed mass suicide rather than surrender. (*Richard Stoneman*)

In AD 78, after he had duly been consul, Agricola was appointed by Vespasian governor of Britain, a job he carried out with efficiency and not a little wisdom.

Vespasian had insight and sense in other directions, too. Though the destruction of Jerusalem and the retaliation against the Jews were carried out with unnecessary severity, and restrictions placed on certain of their practices, Jews were excused Caesar-worship. And in AD 71 he instituted the first salaried public professorship when he appointed Quintilian (AD 40–118) to a chair of literature and rhetoric. He also exempted all doctors and teachers of grammar and rhetoric from paying taxes and from having the military billeted in their homes. Under Vespasian, too, a new class of professional civil servants was created, drawn largely from the business community.

Vespasian died of natural causes and, according to Suetonius, with great dignity, in the family home in the Sabine mountains. On this occasion there were no doubts or worries about the succession.

TITUS

Titus Flavius Sabinus Vespasianus: born on 30 December AD 40 in Rome, son of Vespasian and Flavia Domitilla. Legionary commander and then commander-in-chief in Palestine. Became associate emperor in AD 71, emperor in AD 79. Married [1] Arrecina Tertulla; [2] Marcia Furnilla (one daughter, Flavia Julia). Died on 13 September AD 81. Deified in AD 81.

As early as his boyhood it was clear that he was gifted physically and intellectually, and he became more and more so as he grew up. He was very good-looking, with an authoritative as well as a pleasing manner, and exceptionally strong, though he was short and had a small pot belly. He had an excellent memory and excelled at practically all the arts of war and peace.

(Suetonius, *Titus*, III)

As a young man, Titus was dangerously like Nero in his charm, intellect, lavish ways, and sexual appetite and proclivities. He lived long enough, however, to demonstrate that he had, obviously thanks to the guidance of his father, some talent for government, but not long enough for any judgement to be made as to how effective a ruler he would have been. Yet, in curious ways to which nature has contributed, we have more tangible evidence from his reign of just over two years than from that of many emperors who ruled for much longer.

The massive Arch of Titus, celebrating his triumph over the Jews, still stands in Rome. So does much of the Colosseum, originally known as the Flavian Amphitheatre, begun in AD 72 in the grounds of Nero's Golden Palace and finished in AD 80, the year before Titus's death. Oval in shape and almost 200 metres long and over 150 wide, it housed an arena roughly 75 by 50 metres and could seat some 45,000 spectators. It was the first amphitheatre to be built entirely of stone, and its three tiers of arches, surmounted by pilasters in the Greek style and a deep cornice, provided a model for Renaissance architects. Today tourists wonder and eat pizzas where, in the time of Titus and his successors, men and wild beasts were slaughtered to please the Roman public.

In August AD 79 the volcanic Mount Vesuvius erupted. We have an eye-witness account by Pliny the Younger (AD 61–c. 113), writing to Tacitus:

> To us at a distance, it was not clear which mountain was belching out the cloud, but it was later discovered to be Vesuvius. In form and shape the column of smoke was like a tremendous pine tree, for at the top of its great height it branched out into several skeins. I assume that a sudden burst of wind had carried it upwards and then dropped, leaving it motionless, and that its own weight then spread it outwards. It was sometimes white, sometimes heavy and mottled, as it would be if it had lifted up amounts of earth and ashes.
>
> (*Letters*, VI. 16)

Within an hour or so Pompeii and Herculaneum, among several other towns and villages in the area, were engulfed; many of the survivors managed to escape with the help of the fleet stationed at Misenum, where Pliny was staying. The red-hot ash and lava destroyed, but when it cooled, it preserved, so that modern generations can see what the towns and some of the victims were like at the moment when the disaster struck. Some people suggested that it was divine retribution on Titus for his destruction of Jerusalem. Be that as it may, though he had been emperor for only a few weeks, he immediately announced a state of emergency, set up a relief fund for the homeless, to which was diverted the property of any victims who died intestate, offered practical assistance in rehousing survivors, and appointed a team of commissioners to administer the disaster area.

Titus was twice married; according to Suetonius he divorced his second wife shortly after she gave birth to his only legitimate child, a daughter. While he was in Palestine he had a passionate affair with Berenice, daughter of the Jewish king, Herod Agrippa, and brought her back with him to Rome. The pressure of public opinion, not unmixed with anti-Semitism, forced them apart, and she returned home.

Titus was 40 when he died suddenly. Some people suspected that it was the work of his younger brother, Domitian.

Figure 13   Gold *aureus* (AD 87) of Domitian, with on the reverse Minerva, goddess of crafts and industry, and also of war. The inscription, which begins under the neck and goes clockwise, continuing on the reverse, reads in full: 'The emperor Caesar Domitian Augustus Germanicus, Pontifex Maximus, with powers of a tribune for the sixth time, / Imperator for the fourteenth time, Consul for the thirteenth time, perpetual Censor, Father of the Country'. (×2)

DOMITIAN

Titus Flavius Domitianus Augustus: born on 24 October AD 51 in Rome, younger son of Vespasian and Flavia Domitilla. Became emperor in AD 81. Married Domitia Longina (no children). Murdered on 18 September AD 96.

> From his boyhood he was scarcely polite, being insolent and arrogant in his conversation and behaviour. Once when his father's mistress Caenis came back from Istria and bent forward to kiss him as usual, he offered her his hand instead. . . . He was tall, with a red face, an unassuming expression, and large eyes, though his sight was weak. For all that, he was good-looking, and, especially when he was young, well-proportioned all over, except for his feet; for his toes were slightly deformed. Later on he went bald and developed a paunch.
>
> (Suetonius, *Domitian*, XII, XVIII)

By all accounts, and by the evidence of many of his actions, Domitian was a thoroughly nasty person, but a reasonably effective ruler. First Vespasian, then Titus, kept him at a distance from playing any part in the administration, perhaps to avoid any further suggestions of nepotism, or simply because they felt he did not have the necessary qualities. The public offices which he did hold were largely honorary, and this no doubt soured him. So when supreme power finally came his way, he accepted it as his right and positively gloried in it, especially after arrogating the office of censor, to which he had himself elected for life in AD 85. The usual methods of address were not for him: he preferred to be known as 'our master, our god' (Suetonius, *Domitian*, XIII).

Under the Flavian emperors, the economy of the empire was rationalized further, to the extent that expenditure could at last be projected. Outstanding dependent kingdoms became provinces of Rome. Rome itself and its aristocracy took further strides towards cosmopolitanism. Domitian's contribution was to help these processes by efficient administration, combined with a refreshing pedantry – he insisted on spectators at public games being properly dressed in togas – and a meanness which verged on the neurotic. He was particularly rigorous in exacting from the Jews the tax per head which was statutory throughout the empire, though the historian Flavius Josephus (AD 37–100), who was himself Jewish, suggests that it was imposed by Domitian himself in return for allowing them to practise their own faith. Many Christians were tracked down and made to pay up, on the grounds that in reality they were Jews masquerading as something else. Suetonius records that as a young man he was present in court when a 90-year-old man was publicly examined to ascertain whether he was circumcised.

Domitian was often unsure in handling measures which required initiative. He attempted to resolve the problem of the Italian 'wine lake' by forbidding any new vines to be planted and ordering the destruction of vineyards on the other side of the Alps. Though he was popular with the army – he raised their pay, the first emperor to do so since Augustus – and he had a successful campaign in Germany in AD 83, two or three years later he allowed himself to be deceived into leading his army into battle against a combined force of German tribes who were merely creating a diversion on the Danube, and was heavily defeated. His recall of the popular Agricola from Britain, which had been 'completely conquered and [was] then immediately let go' (Tacitus, *Histories*, I. 2), neither of which statements is supported by the full facts, can be justified from both a military and an economic point of view, as well as on the grounds that Agricola had served as governor for seven years (he was now

44), a very long time for the holder of such a post. Tacitus was of course Agricola's son-in-law: more plausible is his suggestion that Domitian was jealous of Agricola and may have had him poisoned. In his will Agricola named the emperor joint heir with his daughter, Tacitus's wife: 'Domitian's mind was so circumscribed and corrupted by flattery, that he did not see that a good father only makes a ruler his heir if he is a bad one' (Tacitus, *Agricola*, XLIII).

Under Domitian, widespread execution returned. He used a vague charge of *maiestas* (treason) to justify all manner of persecutions and killings, from which members of his own family were not exempt. Conspiracies, real and imaginary, abounded, but Domitian's ultimate murder was not political. It was engineered by his former wife, Domitia, whom he had divorced but was later reconciled with. He was stabbed by a steward, ironically while reading the report of yet another fictitious plot. The senate, no doubt relieved that none of its members was openly involved, was at last in a position to make its own choice of ruler. It nominated a respected lawyer, Marcus Cocceius Nerva (AD 32–98), to take over the government. It was a decision of great significance. Domitian was denied a state funeral, and his name was obliterated from all public buildings.

4

GODS, GODDESSES, AND MYSTERIES

The Romans had a pragmatic attitude to religion, as to most things, which perhaps explains why they themselves had difficulty in taking to the idea of a single, all-seeing, all-powerful god. In so far as they had a religion of their own, any more than they could claim to have an indigenous mythology, it was not based on any central belief, but on a mixture of fragmented rituals, taboos, superstitions, and traditions which they collected over the years from a number of sources. To the Romans, religious faith was less a spiritual experience than a contractual relationship between mankind and the forces which were believed to control people's existence and well-being. The result was essentially two-fold: a state cult whose significant influence on political and military events outlasted the republic, and a private concern, in which the head of the family supervised the domestic rituals and prayers in the same way as the elected representatives of the people performed the public ceremonials. As circumstances and man's view of the world changed, individuals whose personal religious needs remained unsatisfied turned increasingly during the first century AD to the mysteries, which were of Greek origin, and to the cults of the east.

THE ORIGINS OF ROMAN RELIGION

Many of the gods and goddesses worshipped by the Romans were borrowed from the Greeks, or had their equivalents in Greek mythology. Some of these came by way of the Etruscans or the tribes of Latium. The Diana to whom Servius Tullius built the temple on the Aventine Hill was identified with the Greek Artemis, but some of the rites attached to her at Aricia, the

76

centre from which he transferred her worship, went back to an even mistier past. The priest of Diana at Aricia, who was always a runaway slave, held the title of king. He took office by killing his predecessor, and held it for as long as he was able to defeat other runaway slaves in single combat. A fugitive slave could challenge him by breaking off a branch from a particular tree in the sacred grove; so naturally the resident priest kept a close watch.

Some vestiges of earlier magic accompanied Diana to her new site in Rome.

> In the country of the Sabines there was bred on the property of a certain head of family a heifer of astonishing size and perfection of form; to which its horns testified, for they hung in the entrance court of the temple of Diana for many years. The beast was held to be the subject of an omen, as indeed it was: seers prophesied that the state whose citizens sacrificed it to Diana should be the leading power in the land. This prediction came to the notice of the priest of the temple in Rome. On the first day which seemed appropriate for the sacrifice, the Sabine brought the heifer to Rome, drove it to the temple of Diana, and stood with it before the altar. The Roman priest, much impressed by the size of the victim, which was famous, and knowing the prophecy, said to the Sabine: 'What are you doing, stranger? Would you sacrifice to Diana in a state of uncleanliness? You must purify yourself in running water. The Tiber is at the bottom of the valley.' The Sabine, conscious of correct procedure and wanting to do everything by the book so that the prophecy might be fulfilled, immediately went down to the river. While he was away, the priest sacrificed the heifer to Diana, for which the king and his subjects were exceptionally grateful.
>
> (Livy, *History of Rome*, I. 45)

Occasionally tradition threw up a deity whose antecedents had been forgotten. Such a one was the goddess Furrina, who gave her name to the grove in which Gaius Gracchus met his death; her festival was regularly observed on 25 July. Unfortunately, by the middle of the first century BC, no one could remember who she was or why she was being celebrated.

The Romans inherited their preoccupation with examining every natural phenomenon for what it might foretell from the

Figure 14 Sixth- or fifth-century BC Etruscan bronze plaque of a *haruspex* at work; his function was to examine the entrails of sacrificed animals and foretell the future from what he saw. (*C. M. Dixon*)

Etruscans, who had developed the practice if not into a science, then at least into an art. The Etruscans employed three main kinds of divination, which were said to have been communicated to them by a mysterious lad called Tages, who appeared to them having literally been ploughed up from the earth while it was being tilled:

1 Divining the future from examining the entrails of victims sacrificed at the altar – the liver was of particular significance.

2 Observing and explaining the meaning of lightning and advising on how sinister predictions might be averted.
3 Interpreting any unusual phenomena and taking necessary action.

Many primitive societies practised animism, the belief that natural and physical objects are endowed with mystical properties. The Romans took this cult so far that they could be said to have made it peculiarly their own. They invested trees, springs, caves, lakes, animals, even household furniture with *numina* (singular *numen*, meaning 'divine power' or 'spirit'). Stones could have spirits, too, especially the boundary stones between one person's property and the next. The word for a boundary stone was *terminus*; there was even a great god Terminus, a massive piece of masonry which stood permanently in the temple of Jupiter on the Capitoline Hill, because, it was said, it refused to budge even for Jupiter.

PRAYER AND SACRIFICE

The contractual relationship between mankind and the gods involved each party in giving, and in return receiving, services. The Romans believed that spirits residing in natural and physical objects had the power to control the processes of nature, and that man could influence these processes by symbolic action. The first is a primitive form of religious creed; the second is a type of magic.

The 'services' by which Romans hoped to influence the forces that guided their lives were firmly established in ritual – the ritual of prayer and the ritual of offering. In either case, the exact performance of the rite was essential. One slip, and you had to go back to the beginning and start again. The very multiplicity of deities caused problems, as did the gender of some of them: 'whether you be god or goddess' is a common formula in Roman prayers. The poet Horace (65–8 BC) dedicated to Augustus an ode calling for divine assistance to restore the fortunes of Rome, but is clearly in doubt as to whom his appeal should be addressed: 'Upon which of the gods should the people call to revive the failing empire?' (*Odes*, I. 2). He plays safe by starting at the top of the hierarchy: 'To whom will Jupiter assign the task of

Figure 15 Silver statuette of the god Mercury, *c.* AD 150–220, actual size. Mercury, god of merchants and business transactions, is identified with the Greek god, Hermes, herald and messenger of the gods and guide of travellers. He is thus often represented as wearing a *petasus*, the wide-brimmed hat worn by travellers to protect them from the rain and sun.
(*British Museum*)

receiving atonement for our crimes?' He then cites four candidates in turn: Apollo, Venus, Mars, Mercury.

Many Roman deities went by a variety of names, and might not respond if wrongly addressed. So Catullus (*c.* 85–53 BC), in a hymn to Diana (Poem **XXXIV**), is careful also to invoke her as 'Latona's daughter, splendid child of Jove . . . called Juno Lucina by those in childbirth's pangs, and also queenly Trivia, and Luna, she who shines with borrowed light'. The poem ends on a note of respectful exasperation, and with a ritual escape clause: 'Accept our prayer under *any* name by which it pleases you to be addressed.' These lines throw up another identity problem in that Juno Lucina (Lucina here means 'bringing into the light') is not Diana, but Juno, consort of Jupiter, appearing here in her guise as goddess of childbirth. Juno had at least ten other names or surnames for use on special days or in particular circumstances, including Juno Moneta ('Juno the Mint'), because her temple on the Capitoline Hill housed the state mint where money was coined and stored.

There were few occasions on which a prayer was inappropriate. There was a prayer for the return of stolen property and another for the diversion of some unspecified piece of ill-fortune to someone else. Some prayers were realistic and modest, for example Horace's 'Poet's Prayer', which ends: 'I pray, Apollo, let me be content with what I have, enjoy good health and clarity of mind, and in a dignified old age retain the power of verse' (*Odes*, I. 31). This is, however, about the nearest any Roman usually got to praying for anything but material blessings.

Prayer was almost invariably accompanied by some form of offering, or sacrifice. This did not necessarily involve the ritual slaughter of an animal, as long as the offering represented life in some form: it could be millet, cakes made from ears of corn which had been picked a month earlier, fruit, cheese, bowls of wine, or pails of milk. Each deity had his or her own preference — a ram for Janus, a heifer for Jupiter. For Mars it was usually a combination of ox, pig, and sheep, but on 15 October it had to be a race horse. In fact it had to be the winner: the near-side horse of the winning pair in the chariot race that day was immediately taken to the altar and slaughtered. Then its tail was cut off and the blood that dripped from it preserved as a charm. The sex of a chosen animal was also significant: male for gods, female for goddesses. So was its colour. White beasts were offered to deities of the upper world, black to those of the underworld, but a red dog was sacrificed to Robigus, symbolizing the destruction of red mildew.

The sacrificial routine was elaborate and messy. The head of the victim was sprinkled with wine and bits of sacred cake made from flour and salt. Then its throat was cut and it was disembowelled to ensure there was nothing untoward about its entrails. If there was, it was not only a bad omen, but the whole process had to be repeated with a fresh animal until it came out right. The vital organs were burnt upon the altar and the carcase cut into pieces and eaten on the spot, or else laid aside. Then the priest, wearing something over his face to shut out evil influences from his eyes, would say prayers, speaking under his breath,

GODS, GODDESSES, AND SPIRITS

Annona Mythical personification of the annual food supply
Apollo (Greek) God of healing and prophecy
Asclepius (Greek) God of healing
Attis (Phrygian) Beloved of Cybele
Bacchus (Greek as Dionysus) God of wine
Bellona Goddess of war
Bona Dea 'Good Goddess': unnamed spirit whose rites were attended only by women
Cardea Household goddess of door hinges
Castor & Pollux (Greek: also as Dioscuri) Two legendary heroes
Ceres (Identified with Greek Demeter) Goddess of agriculture
Consus God of the granary
Cybele (Phrygian) See Magna Mater
Diana (Identified with Greek Artemis) Goddess of light; also unity of peoples
Dis (Greek as Pluto) God of the underworld
Faunus (Identified with Greek Pan) God of fertility
Flora Goddess of fertility and flowers
Forculus Household god of doors
Fortuna (also Fors, Fors Fortuna) Goddess of good luck
Genius Protecting spirit
Hercules (Greek) God of victory and commercial enterprises
Hermes See Mercury
Isis (Egyptian) Goddess of the earth
Janus God of doorways
Juno (Identified with Greek Hera) Goddess of women
Jupiter (also Jove: identified with Greek Zeus) God of the heavens
Juturna Goddess of fountains
Lar (plural Lares) Spirit of the household
Larvae (or Lemures) Mischievous spirits of the dead
Liber God of fertility and vine-growing
Libitina Goddess of the dead
Limentinus Household god of the threshold
Magna Mater (Phrygian as Cybele) 'Great Mother', goddess of nature

Manes Spirits of the dead

Mars God of war

Mercury (Identified with Greek Hermes) God of merchants

Minerva (Identified with Greek Athena) Goddess of crafts and industry

Mithras (Persian) God of light

Neptune (Greek Poseidon) God of the sea

Nundina Presiding goddess at the purification and naming of children

Ops God of the wealth of the harvest

Osiris (Egyptian) Consort of Isis

Pales God/goddess of shepherds

Penates Household spirits of the store cupboard

Picumnus & Pilumnus Agricultural gods associated with childbirth

Pomona Goddess of fruit

Portunus God of harbours

Priapus God of fertility in gardens and flocks

Quirinus State god under whose name Romulus was worshipped

Robigus God of mildew

Sabazius (Phrygian) God of vegetation

Salus God of health

Sarapis (Egyptian) God of the sky

Saturn (Identified with Greek Cronos) God of sowing

Silvanus God of the woods and fields

Sol God of the sun

Tellus Goddess of the earth

Terminus God of property boundaries

Venus (Identified with Greek Aphrodite) Goddess of love

Vertumnus (also Vortumnus) God of orchards

Vesta (Identified with Greek Hestia) Goddess of the hearth

Volturnus God of the river Tiber

Vulcan God of fire

while a flute was played to drown any ill-omened noise. Any unintentional deviation from the prescribed ritual meant not only a new sacrifice, but an additional one in expiation of the error. The victim in this case was usually a pig. On high occasions, on which a replay of the entire ceremony might be an embarrassment, an expiatory sacrifice was performed as a matter of course on the previous day, in the hope of atoning for any sin of omission or error on the day itself.

Multiple sacrifices were commonplace: the word hecatomb, which derives from the Greek, means the sacrifice of a hundred head of oxen. Human sacrifice was not a usual Roman practice, but was not entirely unknown. In the terrible days which followed the defeat by Hannibal at Cannae in 216 BC, two vestal virgins were convicted of having sexual relations. One was walled up alive, the traditional punishment for this offence; the other committed suicide. Whereupon the *pontifex maximus* got hold of one of the men in the case and personally clubbed him to death. This was regarded as an act not so much of murder as of ill-omen, and recourse was had to the Sibylline Books, the national storehouse of prophetic utterances, for remedies against impending further disasters: 'Among other sacrifices, a Gaulish couple and a Greek couple were walled up alive in the cattle-market, in an underground tomb which had once before [in 228 BC] been stained with human victims, an un-Roman practice' (Livy, *History of Rome*, XXII. 57).

OMENS

A sibyl was a Greek prophetess. The story goes that one of her kind offered to Tarquinius Superbus a collection of prophecies and warnings in the form of nine books at a high price. When he refused, she threw three of them into the fire and offered him the remaining six at the original price of the nine. He refused again; she burned three more and offered him the surviving three, still at the same price. This time he bought them, at what he could have paid for all nine. The Sibylline Books were consulted on the orders of the senate at times of crisis and calamity, in order to learn how the wrath of the gods could be allayed. They were accidentally burned in 83 BC, and envoys were sent all round the known world to collect a set of similar utterances. Augustus had the new collection put in the temple of Apollo on the Palatine

84

GODS, GODDESSES, AND MYSTERIES

Hill, where it remained until it was finally destroyed in the fifth century AD.

Disasters were seen by the Romans as manifestations of divine disapproval, and unusual phenomena as portents of catastrophe. In the winter of 218/217 BC, just before the battle of Trasimene, but with Hannibal already ensconced in Italy, the following portents were said to have been observed:

> In Rome a 6-month-old freeborn infant shouted 'Victory' in the vegetable market; in the cattle market an ox climbed up three flights of stairs on its own and then jumped out of a window in fright when the inhabitants screamed; phantom ships glowed in the sky; the temple of Hope, in the vegetable market, was struck by lightning. In Lanuvium a sacrificial corpse moved and a crow flew down into the temple of Juno and alighted on her sacred couch. In the district of Amiternum, ghostly men in shining garb materialized in many places but did not approach anyone. In Picenum it rained stones. At Caere oracular tablets shrank. In Gaul a wolf stole a sentry's sword from its sheath and ran off with it.
>
> (Livy, *History of Rome*, XXI. 62)

Reports of phenomena such as these could cause panic among a people for whom superstition was a way of life, especially at times of national uncertainty. The Sibylline Books were promptly consulted, except apparently about the case of the raining stones, which it was felt could be dealt with by an official period of nine days' prayer. Various methods of appeasement emerged for the rest, including the ceremonial purging of the entire city of Rome, sacrifices, gifts to temples of Juno of gold ingots (each weighing 40 lb) and bronze statues, and a series of symbolic feasts at which statues of the gods were laid in reclining positions on couches round a banqueting table. At the end of it all, Livy reports, the Roman people felt considerably relieved.

The awe in which the Sibylline Books were held and the reverence with which their revelations were treated illustrate their significance in the Romans' relationship with their gods. The taking of omens or auspices – the literal meaning of the latter is 'signs from birds' – was a standard procedure before any state activity, as is illustrated by the story of the legendary founding of Rome itself. An official augur, who was present on such occasions merely as a consultant, marked out and prepared

85

the statutory square measure of ground and then handed over to the state official who was to perform the ritual. He took up his position and observed the flights of any birds he could see, their kind, height, position, speed, direction of flight. If there was any doubt about the interpretation of what the official saw, the augur was called upon to advise. Later, armies took with them a portable auspice-kit, consisting of a cage of sacred chickens, in front of whom bits of cake were placed to see what would happen. It was a bad sign if they refused to eat: good if they ate the cake and let bits of grain fall from their beaks. The consul Claudius Pulcher, newly arrived in Sicily from Rome to take up his command in 249 BC, 'began a sea-battle though the sacred chickens had refused to eat when he took the auspices. In contempt of religious practice, he threw the chickens into the sea, remarking that if they would not eat they could drink' (Suetonius, *Tiberius*, II). He was very lucky to escape from the ensuing débâcle, during which ninety-three Roman ships and their crews were captured by the Carthaginians.

Public business was frequently interrupted so that the omens could be consulted. A law passed by an assembly or an election could be declared invalid if the correct procedure had not been carried out. There was no need in political assemblies to resort to the tactic of filibustering to obstruct proceedings: religious grounds could suffice. In 59 BC Julius Caesar's consular colleague, the perhaps aptly named Marcus Bibulus, announced that he proposed to offer religious justification for the assemblies to reject Caesar's legislation. Fearful, in the prevailing unrest, of venturing out of his house, he sent messages that he was watching the sky for omens. As bad omens had to be announced in person before the start of business to be valid, this raised an awkward precedent. Caesar overruled Bibulus's tactics, but for some time these particular laws were regarded with suspicion.

There was a distinction between signs that were solicited and those which appeared without invitation. The more startling or unexpected the sign, for instance a sudden flash of lightning or an epileptic fit on the part of a member of an assembly, the more seriously it was taken. It was not unknown for an interested party to throw a feigned fit in order to obstruct proceedings. Lightning which appeared while auspices were being taken was good news: not so when it came unbidden. In 114 BC the unthinkable happened and a vestal virgin was struck by lightning. A special commission was set up which by dubious means procured the conviction of several other vestals for sexual offences. Hysteria was still not abated, and the senate called for a reading from the Sibylline Books. The same answer was returned as just over a century before, and a Greek and a Gallic couple were buried alive.

WORSHIP IN THE HOME

Two national deities had their place in private worship too: Vesta, goddess of the fire and the hearth, and Janus, god of doorways. Janus, who gave his name to the month of January, is often depicted as having two faces, one looking in each direction. For this there are several interpretations: that it represents opening and closing a door, going in and coming out, or viewing (and thus guarding) both the inside and outside of a house. The door itself was so highly regarded that it required the attention of three more deities: Cardea, goddess of hinges; Limentinus, god of the threshold; and Forculus, who presided over the individual leaf or leaves. Vesta was particularly important to the women of the household, for the hearth was where the food was prepared and cooked, and beside it the meal was eaten. Prayers were said to Vesta every day, and during a meal a portion of food might be thrown into the fire as an offering, and also to seek omens from the way in which it burned.

The particular gods of the household were its *lares* and *penates*. The *lares* (one of them was designated *lar familiaris* or 'family spirit' and was special to that household) were supposed to be the spirits of dead ancestors, and had a cupboard of their own which they inhabited in the form of tiny statuettes. Daily prayers and offerings were made to them, with more elaborate ones on the sacred days of each month – the calends, ides, and nones – and on notable occasions such as a birth, wedding, birthday, a departure or return, or the first word spoken by a son of the house. The *penates* looked after the larder, its contents and their replenishment, and also had their own cupboard. The statuettes of the *penates* used to be taken out and put on the table at mealtimes, and were sometimes given the names of particular state gods. When the family moved, its *lares* and *penates* went too.

Each household had in addition its *genius*, whose image was a house-snake. *Genius* might be described as a 'spirit of manhood', since it was supposed to give a man the power of generation, and its particular sphere of influence was the marriage-bed. The household *genius* was especially honoured on the birthday of the head of the family.

Births, marriages, and deaths all had their special rituals. Juno Lucina was, as we have seen, the main deity of childbirth, but there were other spirits who watched over the embryo child and its mother from the moment of conception to the birth itself. Immediately after the birth, a sacred meal was offered to Picumnus and Pilumnus, two jolly rustic deities, for whom a made-up bed was kept in some conjugal bedrooms. A positive string of child-development deities watched over the baby's breast-feeding, bones, posture, drinking, eating, and talking, even its accent. On the ninth day after the birth of a boy, the eighth in the case of a girl, the ceremony of purification and naming was enacted, presided over by the goddess Nundina. Free-born children received an amulet – gold for a child of the rich, bronze or merely leather for poorer families – which a girl would wear until her marriage, and a boy until he exchanged his *toga praetexta*, the robe of a child which was also worn by girls, for the *toga virilis*, the garb of a man, at the age of between 14 and 17.

There were several ways of celebrating a marriage, of which the simplest involved the consent of both parties, without rites or ceremony. There were three others, each giving the husband legal power over his wife:

1 By cohabiting for a year without the woman being absent for more than a total of three nights.
2 By a symbolic form of purchase, in the presence of a holder of a pair of scales and five witnesses.
3 By full ritual, in the presence of the *pontifex maximus*. This was obligatory for patrician families, and comprised a form of religious service with prayer, a bloodless sacrifice, the offering and eating of sacred bread, and the taking of auspices. The bride and bridegroom sat on two chairs bound together and covered with lambskin.

After the second century AD a different kind of ritual emerged, which began with a formal betrothal, at which the prospective bride slipped a gold ring on to the finger now known as the 'wedding finger' in the presence of the guests. For the marriage ceremony itself she wore a veil of flaming orange-red, surmounted by a simple wreath of blossom. There was animal sacrifice and the inevitable examination of the entrails for happy omens, after which the couple exchanged vows and the wedding guests shouted their congratulations.

While a spirit of some kind watched over a person at most times and on most occasions from conception to death, at the actual moment of death there was none. The religious element in the funeral rites was directed towards a symbolic purification of the survivors. After the burial or cremation, a sow was sacrificed to Ceres to cleanse the house, and any refuse in it was solemnly swept out, while the family was sprinkled with water, and then invited to step over a ceremonial fire. After that, everyone sat down to a feast. Once the corpse was buried – and even in the case of cremation one bone was preserved and put in the ground – its own spirit joined all those other spirits of the dead, which were known collectively as *manes* and required regular worship and appeasement. There were also mischievous spirits of the dead, known as *larvae* or *lemures*, which could, however, be exorcized by the master of the house performing an elaborate ritual, involving the spitting out of black beans and the clanking of brass pots.

WORSHIP IN THE FIELDS

To the countryman, the natural world teemed with religious significance. The fields, orchards, vineyards, springs, and woods all had their attendant deities or spirits – every oak-tree, for instance, was sacred to Jupiter. Silvanus, god of the woods and fields, guarded the boundary between farmland and forest, and the estate had regularly to be protected from natural and supernatural hazards by lustration, the ritual of purification involving sacrifice and a solemn procession round its perimeter. The country year was crowded with festivals of appeasement, prayer, and rejoicing.

The farmer's annual round began in the spring, which the original Roman calendar reflected by its year beginning on 15 March. The establishment of what is now New Year's Day in Christian countries at 1 January was for sheer administrative convenience. In 153 BC, in order to enable the arrival in Spain of the incoming consul to coincide with the start of the campaign season, the beginning of his term of office, and thus of the year, was advanced to 1 January, and there it remained. The first celebration of the country year was the Liberalia on 17 March, in honour of Liber, god of fertility in the fields and vineyards. It was also the traditional date on which a teenage boy abandoned his *toga praetexta* for the *toga virilis*.

The latter part of April was a riot of festivals, each with its special significance. At the Fordicia on 15 April, pregnant cows were sacrificed to the earth-goddess Tellus, and in Rome itself foetuses were burned and the ashes kept for use at the festival of the Parilia the following week, at which the sheep were purified by being driven through bales of blazing straw. Ceres, goddess of agriculture and especially of corn, had her festival on 19 April, as Virgil records in his verse handbook on farming, the *Georgics*:

> First thing of all is to revere the gods, especially Ceres: to her greatness dedicate the yearly rites. Perform them on the grass which burgeons at the very end of winter, in the bright days of spring. The lambs are fat, the wine is at its softest, sleep is sweet, and all the shadows thicken on the hills. This is the time when all your country folk should worship Ceres. Mix the mellow wine with milk and honey, lead the sacrifice three times the circle of your new-grown crops, while all your fellow workers follow on behind, chanting and calling Ceres to their homes. Let no one put his sickle to the corn without a wreath of oak-leaves on his head, or giving Ceres an impromptu dance, and singing verses to her bounteousness.
>
> (*Georgics*, I. 338–50)

Here again we have the lustration ritual as an act of purification and bringing of luck. According to Livy, writing of the Macedonian army in 182 BC, there were other ways of achieving the same end:

> A dog is cut in two and the front half placed on the right-hand side of the road, and its rear part, with the entrails, on the left. The army then parades between the two parts in full battle order. At the head of the column are carried the arms and banners of all the kings of Macedonia from its beginnings. Then comes the present king with his children, fol-

lowed by the royal cohort and the king's personal bodyguard, and after them by the troops themselves.

(History of Rome, XI. 6)

In Rome itself, there was a macabre finale to the festival of Ceres. Flaming torches were attached to the tails of foxes, which were let loose in the space below the Capitoline Hill that later became the Circus Maximus. After the Vinalia Rustica, probably a drunken revel to celebrate the end of winter, and the sacrifice of the red dog to Robigus, god of mildew, the month closed with the Floralia, a festival ostensibly to petition for the healthy blossoming of the season's flowers. It lasted from 28 April to 3 May, and appears to have been celebrated with the greatest jollity and licence.

As the crops ripened, there were several rites of a more serious nature, including the movable feast of the Ambarvalia, during which the ritual lustration was renewed and the farmer sacrificed a pig, a sheep, and an ox, together with items from the previous harvest and the first fruits of the new. When the corn was cut in August, there were celebrations to Consus, god of the granary, and Ops, god of harvest wealth, and a further Vinalia Rustica; the real festival of thanksgiving for the wine crop, the Meditrinalia, was observed on 11 October. Sowing took place in December, during which there were repeats of the festivals of Consus and Ops. The Saturnalia was on 17 December. This festival was observed in the country as a genuine celebration of seed-time: in towns it was a longer celebration which embodied some of the secular traditions later associated with Christmas, including holidays from school, candles, exchanges of gifts, the mingling of household staff with the family, and the wearing of party hats.

THE RELIGION OF THE STATE

The religion of the Roman state reflected the ways of private worship, while retaining traditions from the period of the kings. Under the nominal direction of the *pontifex maximus,* administrative and ritualistic matters were the responsibility of four colleges, whose members, with one or two exceptions, were appointed or elected from the ranks of politicians and held office for life.

The members of the Pontifical College, the senior body, were the *rex sacrorum, pontifices, flamines,* and the vestal virgins. *Rex sacrorum* (king of religious rites) was an office created under the early republic to maintain the tradition of royal authority over religious matters. Though in later times he still took precedence at religious ceremonies over all other dignitaries including the *pontifex maximus,* it had by then become largely an honorary position.

The sixteen *pontifices* (priests) were the chief administrators and organizers of the religious affairs of the state, and authorities on procedure and matters of the calendar and festivals, and on the designation of particular days on which certain public business could not be conducted.

The *flamines* were priests of particular gods: three for the major gods, Jupiter, Mars, and Quirinus, and twelve for the lesser ones. These specialists had the technical knowledge of the worship of the particular deity to whom, and to whose temple, they were attached, and performed the daily sacrifice to each. The *flamen dialis* (priest of Jupiter) was the most important of them, and on certain occasions he ranked alongside the *pontifex maximus* and the *rex sacrorum.* His life was hedged around with taboos and hazards. Aulus Gellius recorded, while living in Greece, 'those I can remember'. They included the following:

> He may not ride a horse. . . . If a person is brought into the house of the *flamen dialis* in fetters, he must be untied and the bonds pulled up through the open skylight on to the roof and then let down into the street. . . . Only a free man may cut his hair. It is the custom that the *flamen dialis* may not touch or even mention a nanny-goat, uncooked meat, ivy, or beans. . . . He may not go out without his cap of office; it has only recently been decided by the priests that he can take it off indoors. . . . If he loses his wife, he must resign his office. His marriage cannot be ended except by death.
>
> (*Attic Nights,* X. 15)

The six vestal virgins were chosen from ancient patrician families at an early age to serve at the temple of Vesta. They normally served ten years as novices, the next ten performing the duties, and a further ten teaching the novices. They had their own convent near the forum, and their duties included guarding the sacred fire in the temple, performing the rituals of worship, and baking the salt cake which was used at various festivals throughout the year. Punishment for any lapse in ritual or conduct was rigorous: whipping for letting the sacred fire go out; whipping and being walled up underground, with a few provisions, for a breach of the vow of chastity. The prestige of being a vestal virgin, however, was considerable. She was pre-ceded in the street by a lictor, and any criminal condemned to death who happened to see her passing was automatically reprieved. The disappointment of not being selected appears to have been profound, at least to the girl's parents:

> The emperor [Tiberius in AD 19] then brought up the question of a replacement for Occia, who had for fifty-seven years presided over the rite of Vesta with supreme sanctity. He proposed a vote of thanks to Fonteius Agrippa and Domitius Pollio for the public-spirited way in which they had offered their daughters for selection. Pollio's child had been chosen, for no other reason than that her mother was still living with her husband; Agrippa had divided his house-hold by his divorce. The emperor, however, gave the rejected candidate a surety of a dowry of a million sesterces as a consolation prize.
>
> (Tacitus, *Annals*, II. 86)

The fifteen members of the College of Augurs exercised great learning, and presumably also diplomacy, in the interpretation of omens in public and private life, and acted as consultants in cases of doubt. Each carried a crooked staff, without any knot in it, with which he marked out the square space of ground from which official auspices were observed.

The members of the College of 'Quindecemviri Sacris Faciun-dis' (Fifteen for Special Religious Duties) were the keepers of the Sibylline Books, which they consulted and interpreted when requested to do so, and ensured that any actions prescribed were properly carried out. They also had responsibility for supervising the worship of any foreign deity which was intro-duced into the religion of the state from time to time, usually on the recommendation of the Sibylline Books. Such a one was Cybele, the Phrygian goddess of nature, whose presence in Rome in the form of a sacred slab of black meteoric rock was recommended in 204 BC after, as Livy records, it had rained stones more often than usual. The cult itself, symbolized by noisy processions of attendant eunuch priests and flagellants, was exotic and extreme, in direct contrast to the stately, methodical practices of state religion; Roman citizens were discouraged from participating in its rites until the time of Claudius. The annual public games, however, in honour of Cybele, the 'Great Mother', were held in considerable style from 4 to 10 April, and were preceded by a ceremonial washing and polishing of her stone by members of the college.

The three, later seven, office-holders of the College of 'Epulones' (Banqueting Managers), belonged to the smallest and most junior of the four colleges. It was founded in 196 BC, presumably as a result of the amount of organization required to put on the official feasts which had become integral parts of the major festivals and games. A day each, for instance, was allocated to the public banquets in honour of Jupiter which took place during the Great Roman Games in September and the People's Games in November.

The earliest state religious festivals were celebrated with games, such as the very first one recorded at Rome, the festival to Consus at which the Sabine women were kidnapped. The Consualia, traditionally celebrated in Rome on 21 August, was also the local Derby Day, the main event of the chariot-racing calendar. Whether it was a case of cause or effect, the underground granary, which housed the sacred shrine of Consus where the opening sacrifice was conducted, was conveniently situated in the middle of the Circus Maximus, where the racing took place. Another of the original racing-festivals was the Equirria to Mars on 15 October, this time on the Campus Martius, with its grisly climax that has already been described.

Religious festivals could be grave as well as joyful. February saw both kinds. During the nine days of the Parentilia, during which the family dead were worshipped, state officials did no business, temples were closed, and marriages forbidden. In complete contrast was the ancient and somewhat gruesome Lupercalia, at which the deity honoured was probably Faunus, god of fertility, but the proceedings reflected the origins of Rome itself. They started in the cave where Romulus and Remus were supposed to have been suckled by the wolf. Several goats and a dog were sacrificed, and the blood smeared over two youths of noble family. The pair then ran a prescribed cross-country course, wearing goatskins and carrying strips of hide, with which they whipped people as they passed. The blows were supposed to promote fertility, and women wanting to become pregnant would place themselves at strategic points on the course to receive their stripes.

The marathon festivities for Mars from 1 to 19 March were even more exhausting for the participants. Two teams each of twelve celebrants known as *salii* (jumpers) put on the helmets, uniform, and armour of Bronze Age warriors and leapt through the streets, chanting and beating their shields. Each night they rested, and feasted, at a prearranged hostelry or private house.

The festival of Vesta in June was a more sedate and dignified affair. For a week, the storehouse of treasures in the temple was open to the public (but to married women only), who came barefooted with offerings of food. On 15 June the vestal virgins swept the place out, and public business, which had been suspended during the festival, was resumed. As an extra touch, on 9 June mill-donkeys were hung with garlands of violets, decorated with loaves of bread, and given the day off. There was not a month in the Roman calendar which did not have its religious festivals. August, the sixth month of the old calendar, hosted, in addition to the Consualia, festivals to Hercules (god not just of victory but also of enterprise in business), Portunus (god of harbours), Vulcan (god of fire), and Volturnus (god of the river Tiber). It was the month, too, in which the ancient festival of Diana was remembered on the Aventine.

That January should find itself the first month in the revised calendar was entirely appropriate. Janus, who gave his name to it, was a god unique to the Romans and has no equivalent in any other mythology. He was the god of beginnings as well as of the door, which you meet when you first enter a house. He not only began the year, and received the first state sacrifice of the year at the Agonia on 9 January, but the first hour of the day was sacred to him, and his name took precedence over all others in prayers. His bearded, double-headed image appeared on the first round bronze coin of the republic, the basic *as*, in about 300 BC, and also on the earliest silver coins, minted in Capua. The gates of his temple in the north-east corner of the forum were, it is said on the orders of Numa, kept wide open in times of war. According to Livy, this meant that they were closed only twice in the succeeding seven centuries.

UNDER THE EMPIRE

The survival of a religious faith depends on a continual renewal and affirmation of its beliefs, and sometimes on adapting its ritual to changes in social conditions and attitudes: expansion is possible only through active and organized proselytizing, and by the relevance of its teachings to those to whose attention it is brought. To the Romans, the observance of religious rites was a public duty rather than a private impulse. Their beliefs were founded on a variety of unconnected and often inconsistent mythological traditions, many of them derived from Greek rather than Italian models. Without any basic creed to counter, foreign religions made inroads into a society whose class-structure was being blurred and whose constitution was being changed by the increased presence of freed slaves and of incomers from abroad. The brilliance of some of the major foreign cults had considerable attraction for those brought up on homespun deities of the hearth and fields. The first of these to reach Rome was that of Cybele, according to Livy in 204 BC. The worship of Mithras, the emissary of light who symbolized the fight to disseminate life-giving forces in the face of the powers of darkness and disorder, reached Rome from Persia in the first century AD and had a particular appeal to the army. The fusion of east and west is dramatically illustrated by Tacitus, describing the preliminaries to the second battle of Cremona during the civil war in AD 69. After Antonius Primus, leader of Vespasian's faction, had harangued his troops, 'There was a shout from the whole army, and the men of the Third Legion turned to the east and saluted the rising sun, in accordance with the custom in Syria' (*Histories*, III. 24).

The worship of the Egyptian goddess Isis came to Rome in the early years of the first century BC. Its significance is powerfully reflected in the fictional prose narrative *Metamorphoses* (also known as *The Golden Ass*) by Lucius Apuleius (*fl. c.* AD 160), who became a priest of Isis and her consort Osiris. The protagonist, also called Lucius, is accidentally turned into an ass; after several adventures and misadventures he appeals for help to Isis, having realized the omnipotence of the 'supreme goddess'. She duly appears to him:

> I come in answer to your prayers, Lucius: I, mother nature, ruler of all the elements, original child of time, most power-

ful of divine spirits, queen of the dead, supreme in the heavens, the single face of all gods and goddesses. With a nod I arrange the glowing arch of the sky, the healthy sea breezes, the bitter silence of the underworld. I am one god, worshipped throughout the world in many forms, with different rites, and under a variety of names. . . . The Egyptians, who are skilled in ancient lore, celebrate my being with forms of worship which are unique to me and address me by my real name, Queen Isis.

(*Metamorphoses*, XI. 5)

This is not just a description of a powerful deity, or even of a chief divine: it is an expression of monotheism.

The worship of Isis in the Roman empire was just one of the cults known as 'mysteries', which were of Greek origin. The mysteries based on Eleusis, and those of Cybele and Bacchus, were also significant. They all have in common a ceremony of purification of the initiate, a sense of personal relationship with the deity, and an understanding of a life beyond death. Of the ultimate rite of initiation into the mysteries of Isis, Lucius of the *Metamorphoses* of Apuleius protests:

Perhaps, interested reader, you want to know what was said and done. I would tell you if it was permitted to do so: you would learn if you were permitted to listen. . . . But since you have, for all I know, a religious justification for your curiosity, I will not keep you in an agony of suspense. Listen, now, but believe: this is all true. I travelled to the verge of death, I trod on Proserpina's threshold, I was borne through all the elements, and returned. In the middle of the night I gazed on the sun, dazzlingly clear; I approached the gods of the underworld and the gods of the heavens above, and I worshipped them from so near that I could have touched them.

There now: I have told you what you are forbidden to know, though you have heard it.

(*Metamorphoses*, XI. 23)

The mysteries were cults whose rituals were known only to initiates, who appear closely to have guarded the secrets of them – as well they might, considering the restrictions on any worship which conflicted with that of the state. What do remain, how-

ever, apart from literary allusions, are fascinating glimpses, preserved by nature in the lava from the eruption of Vesuvius in AD 79, of the cults of Isis and Bacchus, in the form of wall paintings uncovered at and near Pompeii.

Traditional beliefs were further eroded in the face of the Greek school of philosophy, the Stoics, who were projecting the notion of a single deity. They were also affected by the Jewish diaspora. A Jewish force assisted Julius Caesar in Egypt during his campaign against Pompey, and he in return granted the Jews privileges which included freedom of worship in Rome itself. Many people responded to an acceptable and assimilable creed, much of whose tradition was based on sound medical practice. A form of semi-Judaism became fashionable, especially among women: one did not have to be a full convert to attend services in synagogues. Hadrian, who became emperor in AD 117, tried to eradicate Judaism by forbidding all Jewish practices. His successor Antoninus, in about AD 138, rescinded Hadrian's legislation, with the significant exception of circumcision, which was restricted to those of the Jewish race. Thus ended widespread proselytism.

Augustus, as a part of his national morale-boosting campaign, reaffirmed the traditional forms of worship. He restored eighty-two temples in and around Rome, it is claimed all in the space of one year, and in 12 BC had himself appointed *pontifex maximus*, a post which thereafter was restricted to emperors. Thus the head of state was once again the head also of religious affairs. He especially promoted the god Apollo, with whom his own family was said to have special affinities, to the status of a major deity,

← *Figure 16* The 'Villa of the Mysteries' at Pompeii was built in the middle of the second century BC and remodelled and redecorated in about 60 BC. One hall of it carries round its walls a continuous series of paintings in bright tones in which the only male figure is a small naked boy. It has been taken to symbolize the preparations of a bride for marriage, while reflecting elements which have been associated with the mysteries of Dionysus (Bacchus). In this section, which goes round a corner, a kneeling woman (left) begins to uncover an object which has been guessed to be an enormous phallus. Next, a winged female figure raises a whip to strike a half-naked girl whose back is being bared by the woman in whose lap she buries her face. On the right a clothed woman holds the *thyrsus*, the wand carried by Bacchus and his adherents, while her naked companion, clashing cymbals above her head, dances in ecstasy. (*C. M. Dixon*) and dedicated a magnificent new temple to him on a site on the Palatine Hill which was his personal property. He did not take the connection between religion and rule so far as to allow himself officially to be regarded as a god in his own lifetime, but he prepared the way to being deified after his death by confirming the divinity of Julius Caesar and dedicating a temple to him. Even one of the most pragmatic of his successors, Vespasian, dedicated new temples to Claudius, Glory and Courage, and Peace.

In about AD 30, in the reign of Tiberius, a young Jewish thinker and teacher, son of a carpenter in Nazareth, was executed in Jerusalem under Roman law. His name was Jesus, and he was held to be the Messiah. While his death was hardly noticed by Roman historians, with hindsight it is perhaps not so remarkable that the first adherents to a new and personalized religion, which had its roots and basic teachings in intellectually the most acceptable faith of the times, should have succeeded in spreading its message through the ancient world. This was especially the case among the lower orders, for whom this new faith seemed to offer a bond of unity with one another, and a means of worshipping a single spiritual god by giving honour to a being with whom they could identify.

During the second century AD Christians were persecuted for

Figure 17 Silver spoons with, in the bowl, early Christian motifs: the chi–rho (χρ) monogram, the first two letters of the Greek word for Christ, flanked by the letters alpha (α) and omega (ω), the first and last letters of the Greek alphabet, signifying the beginning and the end. The Mildenhall Treasure, to which they belong, was unearthed in Suffolk, and was probably brought in by the Christian general Lupicinus, master of the Roman cavalry in Gaul, who was posted to Britain with a force in AD 360. (*British Museum*)

their beliefs largely because these did not allow them to give the statutory reverence to the images of the gods and of the emperor, and because their act of worship transgressed the edict of Trajan forbidding meetings of secret societies. To the government, it was civil disobedience: to the Christians themselves it was the suppression of their freedom of worship. Pliny the Younger, as governor of Bithynia in AD 111, was so exercised by the anomalies on both sides that he wrote to Trajan asking for guidance. Trajan replied:

> The actions you have taken, my dear Pliny, in investigating the cases of those brought before you as Christians, are correct. It is impossible to lay down a general rule which can apply to particular cases. Do not go looking for Christians. If they are brought before you and the charge is proven, they must be punished; with the proviso that if someone denies they are Christian and gives proof of it, by offering reverence to our gods, they shall be acquitted on the grounds of repentance even if they have previously incurred suspicion. Anonymous written accusations shall be disregarded as evidence. They set a bad example which is contrary to the spirit of our times.
>
> (Pliny, *Letters*, X. 97)

Just as the Roman priesthood was a political office, so the religion and the political interests of the state continued in close relationship well into the Christian era.

5

DAILY LIFE, WORK, AND
ENTERTAINMENT

The mass of the population of Rome had welfare benefits of a kind and on a scale never matched before and hardly since, even in Germany under Hitler's cunning régime in the years leading up to the Second World War. The hard and menial work was done by slaves. Leisure hours were comparatively long and leisure pursuits subsidized. Public holidays were plentiful and public entertainment was free. In the times of Julius Caesar and Augustus, 150,000 of the inhabitants of Rome received free grain. Nero was in the habit of handing out gifts of astonishing value and variety:

> Every day all manner of free gifts were thrown to the people: on a single day 1,000 birds of different kinds, a variety of food parcels, and tokens for corn, clothing, gold, silver, jewellery, pearls, paintings, slaves, farm beasts, even wild animals, as well as ships, tenement blocks, and agricultural land.
>
> (Suetonius, *Nero*, **XI**)

The economy of ancient Rome was an issue of the greatest complexity, and Roman numerals were not in any case designed for easy computation. Imports into Italy, especially of wheat, olive oil, and wine were astronomical, as were those of luxury goods from other parts of the Roman world. Consumer spending was restricted in that so many of the population were slaves, and others, especially in Rome itself, were on the dole; while the army, whose presence anywhere had the effect of boosting the local economy, was spread around the provinces. The provinces themselves were meant both to be self-supporting and to provide the fiscal treasury with taxes, as well as to supply Rome with

Figure 18   The frequent appearance of Ceres (with her ears of corn) on the reverse of coins has a double significance. She was an important deity in that according to Virgil in the *Georgics* she taught the Romans to plough and thus to be able to supplement (and later replace) their diet of acorns with wheat; in imperial times the people demanded corn as their right, and many received tokens for free issues. (Bronze *sestertius* of *c.* AD 120,)(2)

staple goods. Some of them were more successful at this than others. There was mass-production of pottery, especially the distinctive and often decorated red-coated bowls, plates, serving dishes, cups, and lamps that have been found even on sites of dwellings of the rural poor. Archaeological evidence has further revealed that branches of Italian potteries began to operate in Germany and Gaul, which then became major manufacturing countries in their own right, exporting their wares to other provinces, and even back to Italy.

Vast sums were expended on public works and entertainments, and on the armed forces. At the end of the day, the emperor was usually blamed for shortages, shortfalls, and anything else to do with the economy.

[In AD 32] the exorbitant price of corn almost led to rioting; as it was, there were frantic demands made in the theatre for several days, even more outspoken against the emperor

Figure 19   The basic coinage instituted by Augustus comprised the copper *quadrans*, brass *semis*, copper *as*, brass *dupondius* and *sestertius*, silver *denarius*, and gold *aureus*. Other coins were introduced from time to time to meet inflation. Constantine replaced the *aureus* with the gold *solidus*. a) *quadrans* of Nero (reverse), with laurel branch; the smallest coin, it is frequently mentioned as the entrance fee to the public baths. b) *semis* of Domitian (= 2 *quadrantes*). c) *as* of Vespasian (= 2 *semisses*). d) *dupondius* of Marcus Aurelius (= 2 *asses*). e) *sestertius* of Hadrian (= 2 *dupondii*). f) *denarius* of Julius Caesar, the first living person to be depicted on a Roman coin (= 4 *sestertii*). g) *aureus* of Augustus (= 25 *denarii*). h) *solidus* of Zeno, emperor in the east at the time of the end of the western empire. Portraits on coins of the later empire reflect eastern influence and have less personality than those of earlier times. (All actual size)

[Tiberius] than was customary. Stung by these, he reprimanded the state officials and the senate for failing to use their authority to control the people, listing the provinces from which he had obtained corn and emphasizing that he had imported greater quantities than Augustus. In response the senate drafted a statement censuring the people in old-fashioned terms of severity, and the consuls issued one which was equally tough. Tiberius's public silence on the matter was not, as he thought, regarded as a constitutionally tactful move, but as arrogance.

(Tacitus, *Annals*, VI. 13)

The emperor always had, however, considerable resources of his own to draw on, particularly from estates which were bequeathed to him or acquired by other means – according to Pliny the Elder, Nero confiscated the entire properties of six men who between them owned almost all the corn land in North Africa, and these were still being cultivated as imperial possessions under the rule of Hadrian, sixty years later. The whole of Egypt, too, had from the time of Augustus constituted an imperial perquisite, in that he had (in his estimation) acquired it by right, and he passed on to his successors the tradition that the ruler owned the land and those who worked it were his tenants. Nerva and his immediate successors, Trajan, Hadrian, Antoninus, and Marcus Aurelius, inherited from Domitian and his father the habit of moderation in personal expenditure. During their rule, however, there was considerable improvement in the provision of roads and harbours, central government money was granted for new buildings in the provinces, and new public assistance programmes were introduced, particularly for the children of poor families in the municipalities, and increased allowances of wine and olive oil, as well as of corn, made to the public in Rome. The successful conclusion of Trajan's invasion of Dacia, begun in AD 101, and especially the output of the Dacian gold and silver mines, boosted the imperial exchequer, but it needed a period of comparative peace, and the careful and dedicated attention of Antoninus and Marcus Aurelius to the levying and collecting of taxes, before comparative liquidity was finally, but only temporarily, achieved.

WORK

Romans rose early and usually worked a six-hour day. The woman's place was firmly in the home: even queuing for the little wooden token entitling a family to the monthly corn dole appears to have been a male prerogative. Free men and freedmen who had work were out and about on their business for the whole morning, contributing to the noise and bustle of urban activity, of which the epigrammatist Martial (AD 40–104) wrote:

105

Figure 20   Mosaic from Ostia, the port of Rome, showing an amphora of wine being loaded on board. Roman merchant ships had a single mast amidships supporting a rectangular sail, and were steered by an oar at the stern. If it had no other cargo, a ship might well carry 6,000 amphorae in layers, each weighing 50 kilos. (*Richard Stoneman*)

'There's no place in Rome for a poor man to think or rest. Schoolmasters disturb life in the morning, bakers at night, while the coppersmiths hammer all day long' (*Epigrams*, XII. 57). The import business was centred on Ostia, where goods from overseas were unloaded, checked, and stored in warehouses before being transferred to barges for the journey upstream. The building industry accounted for a continual supply of skilled labour in the form of architects, surveyors, supervisors, foremen, sculptors, stonemasons, carpenters, and brickworks' managers. In the cities and towns, wholesale and retail markets operated, craftsmen plied their trades, and the little shops, taverns, and inns did their business. They in their turn were supplied with raw materials and foodstuffs by the agricultural estates.

Sons tended to follow the trades of their fathers. Apart from the army, the only respectable callings for the upper classes were the law and politics, since so many professional posts in such fields as architecture, medicine, surgery, dentistry, teaching, and agricultural management were held by freedmen. This left a sizeable group of educated, if not always aristocratic, unemployed, many of whom pursued the occupation of client. Queues of them formed at dawn at the houses of the rich, waiting patiently in their best clothes for some pathetic gift of money or food, which the patron solemnly dispensed to each in order of social seniority.

> Now the toga-clad mob compete for the little baskets of hand-outs on the doorstep. Your patron, however, first looks you in the face, anxious to avoid the fraudsters who give false names; if he recognizes you, you'll get your dole. Then he tells his crier to call the noble-blooded sons of Troy, for they, too, block the doorway, just like us. 'The praetor first, and after him the tribune.' But a freedman is at the head of the queue. 'I was here first,' he complains to deaf ears. 'Why should I be frightened off or be denied my place?'
>
> (Juvenal, *Satires*, I. 95–102)

The more humble or poorer clients would do the rounds of patrons to collect as many donations as possible. That done, the client returned to his writing, if he was a poet like Martial, or mingled with the crowds in the forum or market, which were as much meeting places as centres of public or private business, read the daily newspaper which was posted up in various public spots, or took an early bath. For after work, for women as well as men, a visit to the public baths was usually the order of the day. For the better-off poet, or one such as Horace who boasted a generous patron, the day was less active:

> I lie in until 8 o'clock, then take a walk or, after reading or writing something which will satisfy me during times of contemplation, rub myself down with oil. . . . But when the noonday sun tells my exhausted frame that it is time for the baths, I avoid the Campus and the game of ball. After a light lunch, enough to prevent my having to last out the day on an empty stomach, I loaf around at home.
>
> (*Satires*, I. 6, 122–8)

THE PLACE OF WOMEN

'Our ancestors, in their wisdom, considered that all women, because of their innate weakness, should be under the control

of guardians' (Cicero, *Pro Murena*, XII). The guardian might be
the father, husband, or a male relative, or someone appointed by
the will of the father or husband, or by an official of the state.
The only exceptions up until the time of Augustus were the six
vestal virgins; after Augustus the rule was relaxed in cases of
freeborn women who had had three children and freedwomen
who had had four, provided that there was no father or husband
to exercise control.

It was customary for marriages to be arranged. Pliny the
Younger wrote to a friend about one which, sadly, had to be
cancelled.

> She was only 13, but she had the wisdom of an older woman
> and a matronly dignity, combined with the sweet nature of a
> girl and the innocence of a maiden. . . . She was engaged to
> an excellent young man; the wedding day was fixed and we
> had all been invited. . . . I cannot express in words my
> heartfelt despair when I heard her father (grief finding ever
> more ways of increasing sorrow) laying out on incense,
> perfumes, and spices for her funeral what he had budgeted
> for gowns, pearls, and jewellery for her wedding.
>
> *(Letters,* V. 16)

Nothing, it seems, was a woman's own.

> Your maidenhead is not entirely yours: a third belongs to
> your father, and a third to your mother. You own the rest.
> Don't resist your parents: they have handed over their rights
> of guardianship to their son-in-law, together with your
> dowry.
>
> (Catullus, Poem LXII. 63–6)

The size of the dowry was expected to match the social
standing of the prospective bridegroom.

TO QUINTILIAN
Though you yourself have few needs and have brought up
your daughter as befits a child of yours and a grandchild of
Tutilius, she is, however, to be married to a man of great
distinction, Nonius Celer, whose status in the community
demands a certain ostentation by way of gowns and attendants (not that these enhance a bride's value, only show it off
to its best advantage). Now I know that you are not blessed

with as much wealth as you are with intellect. So I am taking upon myself part of your responsibility and, in the capacity of an additional father, propose to settle on our girl fifty thousand sesterces. It would be more, but I reckon only an insignificant sum could prevail over your modesty and, that being so, you will not refuse it. Yours.

(Pliny the Younger, *Letters*, VI. 32)

In the history of letter writing, there can be few to match this one for tact as well as generosity.

Women in Roman times, though discriminated against, and subjected to abuse by such poets as Horace and Juvenal (*c.* AD 55–*c.* 140), were still capable of standing up for themselves when aroused. One of the most contentious pieces of Roman legislation was the Oppian Law, brought in after the defeat by Hannibal at Cannae in 216 BC with the object of reducing spending on luxury goods. Livy picks up the story when describing events of the year 195 BC.

In between concerns of great wars either just finished or about to begin, there occurred an incident which is brief enough to record but which, because of the intensity it generated, blew up into a major confrontation. The tribunes of the people Marcus Fundanius and Lucius Valerius proposed to the [tribal] assembly the repealing of the Oppian Law, sponsored during the consulship of Quintus Fabius and Tiberius Sempronius by the tribune Gaius Oppius at the height of the Punic War, whereby no woman could possess more than half an ounce of gold, or wear a dress dyed in a variety of colours, or ride in a horse-drawn carriage in a city or town or within a mile of it except on holy days. The tribunes Marcus and Publius Junius Brutus were for keeping the law and announced they would veto its repeal. Many representatives of the nobility rose to speak for the ayes or the noes. The Capitol was packed with voters in favour or against. Neither modesty nor the persuasion or authority of their husbands could keep the women indoors. They blocked all the streets and entrances to the forum, vociferously arguing that at a time of prosperity, when men's personal fortunes were increasing daily, women too should be restored to their former splendours. The press of women increased day by day, as they came in from the towns and outlying districts. They even grew so bold as to waylay and interrogate the consuls, praetors, and other officials.

(*History of Rome*, XXXIV. 1)

There was a prolonged and impassioned debate, during which Cato the Elder, needless to say, spoke against the motion.

The next day an even greater crowd of women poured out of their houses into the streets, and mass-picketed all the entrances to the homes of the two Brutuses, who had announced that they were vetoing their colleagues' proposal. Nor would they let up until the tribunes agreed to withdraw the veto. There was now no doubt that all the tribes would vote for the motion: the law was duly rescinded, twenty years after it had first been passed.

(*History of Rome*, XXXIV. 8)

In such a restricted environment it is not surprising that, except for the obvious callings and those for which women only are fitted or to which they are more suited than men, there seem to have been a comparatively small number of them in professional jobs. There are, however, records of a few female doctors, clerks, and secretaries; also hairdressers, for whom training was obligatory, teachers, and the occasional fishmonger, vegetable seller, dressmaker, and wool or silk merchant. There were certainly female gladiators: Martial makes a point of mentioning them in his book celebrating the shows put on by Titus in AD 80 in the recently completed Colosseum:

You demand more, Caesar, than to be served under unconquerable arms by warlike Mars: Venus herself is also at your command.

Noble tradition tells how Hercules slew the lion in the wastes of the Nemean valley. Let the ancient tale be reduced to silence: after your shows, Caesar, we can say that we have seen such deeds performed by a woman's hand.

(*Spectacles*, VII, VIII)

It would seem, from a relief now in the British Museum, that when women fought each other in the arena, they did not wear helmets.

Women were expected to possess to a considerable degree that essentially Roman quality of *pietas*, which is untranslatable except as a combination of duty, devotion, and loyalty, especially to the gods, and to one's parents, husband, relations, and country. None displayed it more sublimely than Pompeia Paulina, young wife of the aged Seneca, when Nero's men came to order him to commit suicide while he was at dinner with her and two friends. After asking for, and being refused, the tablets comprising his will, he commended himself to his friends, made a few guarded comments about Nero's habitual cruelty, and embraced his wife.

> He asked her, entreated her, to temper her grief, and not to allow it to be a permanent burden; rather to take genuine consolation for the loss of her husband in the contemplation of his virtuous life. Paulina assured him that she had every intention of dying with him, and demanded a share of the fatal knife. Seneca, by no means averse to her having her moment of glory, and at the same time moved by an affection which would not allow him to risk exposing to possible outrage someone he loved so deeply, said: 'I offered you the comfort of life: you have chosen the dignity of death. I shall not deny you the chance to show such an example. May the steadfastness of such a brave ending bring honour to us both, but the greater fame be accorded to your death.' Then they sliced open the veins in their arms with a single stroke of the knife.
>
> (Tacitus, *Annals*, XV. 63)

That, however, was by no means the end of the story. Because of Seneca's age and the spareness of his frame (the result of 'frugal living'), his blood was so sluggish that he had to cut open the veins in his legs, too. After persuading Paulina, streaming with her own blood, to retire into another room, he dictated a long statement to his secretaries, and then ordered his doctor to administer poison to him. When this did not do the trick, he had himself lifted into a hot bath and was asphyxiated by the steam.

Meanwhile Nero, hearing what had happened and being unwilling to be held responsible for the death also of Paulina, gave orders that she should be revived. While soldiers stood over them, her staff bandaged her arms and staunched the bleeding. She lived a few years longer, 'faithful to her husband's memory to a most praiseworthy degree, the pallor of her face and body

testifying to the extent to which her soul had been destroyed'
(Tacitus, *Annals*, XV. 64).

Certainly women were able to attain a degree of education
and to absorb and reflect the culture of the times. Some even
had some fun, as well as influence: notably Sempronia, whom
Catiline earmarked as a potential recruit to his revolutionary
cause in 63 BC.

> She used to behave with the outrageous audacity of a man.
> Yet this woman was of an excellent family, and was blessed
> with beauty, and then with a husband and children. She had
> studied Greek and Latin literature; she sang to her own
> accompaniment on the lyre; she danced more gracefully
> than a respectable woman needs to do, and had many
> other superfluous gifts. But there was nothing she respected
> less than decorum or modesty. It was not easy to decide
> whether she was more spendthrift with her money or her
> reputation. She was so oversexed that she made passes at
> men more often than they did at her. She often broke
> promises, reneged on debts, and was an accessory to mur-
> der; she would get herself into deep trouble because of both
> her luxurious living and her lack of cash. Yet she was a
> woman of ability: she wrote poetry; she was witty; her
> conversation could be modest, sympathetic, or provocative.
> She was, in fact, an exceedingly amusing and charming
> person.
>
> (Sallust, *The Conspiracy of Catiline*, XXVI)

SLAVES

In using slave labour, the Romans were perpetuating an institu-
tion which had existed in Egypt since at least 2600 BC, and had
been carried on under the empires of China, India, Babylon,
and by the Greeks. Nor does it seem that the treatment of the
slaves who worked the vast farmlands of Italy was very much
harsher than or different from that meted out to African slaves
on the American and West Indian plantations in the eighteenth
century, or that the majority of household slaves were worse off
than many domestic staff in Europe at an even later date. The
Romans, however, especially after the gradual decline of peasant
farming in Italy from about 200 BC, based much of the social and

economic fabric of their empire on slavery. When attitudes changed, fuelled partly by Christianity, which was not so much anti-slavery as pro-benevolence, and the supply of slaves from abroad dwindled, that part of the fabric began to disintegrate. By the end of the second century AD, emancipated slaves were joining the free-born poor in the struggle for existence.

One of the functions of official provincial tax-collectors, especially in Asia Minor, was to kidnap potential slaves and ship them to the specialist slave-markets, one of the biggest of which, at Delos, could process 10,000 slaves in a day. Acquisition of slaves by conquest was a standard practice. Julius Caesar records laconically of one of his campaigns of aggression: 'The next day the gates were broken down, there being no one to defend them, and the troops marched in. Caesar sold off a district of the town lock, stock, and barrel. The dealers gave him a receipt for 53,000 head of people' (*Gallic War*, II. 33). It is questionable, however, whether his behaviour on that day was more inhuman than on another similar occasion:

> Caesar, aware that his compassion was widely recognized, was not at all concerned that harsher treatment of the inhabitants of the town might be regarded as innate brutality, but at the same time he could not see any satisfactory outcome of his plans if more of the population in other parts of the country took the same action. He therefore decided to make an example of them to deter the rest. He spared the lives of those who had taken up arms against him, but cut off their hands, a punishment intended clearly to demonstrate the evil of their ways.
>
> (*Gallic War*, VIII. 44)

Until the empire, marriage between slaves was not recognized, and their children automatically assumed the status of slave. A slave could keep what he could save towards buying his freedom, but if he ran away and was caught, the punishment was branding or death. There was hardly any aspect of daily life, or of work or the leisure industry, in which slaves were not involved, and their treatment, which was entirely the responsibility of their owner, varied according to their skills and the labour which was required of them. They were trained to fight each other, and wild animals, to the death in the arenas of the empire; it was from a training establishment for gladiators that Spartacus the

Thracian led out a band of slaves and in 73 BC began his two-year campaign of revolt. During the later republic, gangs of slaves worked in fetters on the agricultural estates and were chained up in semi-underground barracks at night. Others did not suffer so much. Great numbers of herdsmen were required, and in 8 BC Gaius Caecilius Isodorus, himself a former slave, left a staff of 4,116, most of whom would have been employed in this capacity. Cato the Elder, who acquired young slaves as an investment and sold them at a profit after training, laid down that a staff of twelve (a manager, his wife, and eleven hands) was the right number to work a farm of 150 acres devoted to olive-growing and sheep. There is little doubt that Roman technology could have devised many labour-saving devices, particularly for use on the farm, were it not that an abundance of slave labour was an economic fact of life.

Slaves worked in the mines, and also in the potteries. They constituted the state's labour force for building and maintaining public works, and in other government services such as the mint and the corn supply; they were also its 'white-collar' workers, who kept the machinery of bureaucracy and administration working. They served as clerks and accountants in private businesses, and as secretaries, teachers, librarians, doctors, scribes, artists, and entertainers. And they constituted the private staff of villas, town houses, and palaces. Household slaves had perquisites – even in the house of the bombastic and vulgar freedman Trimalchio, portrayed in Gaius Petronius's novel, *Satyricon*, they got what was left over from the dinner-party. Some, however, suffered unusually severe hazards:

> Vedius Pollio, Roman knight and a friend of the divine Augustus, practised his barbarity with the assistance of moray eels, into whose tanks he threw condemned slaves: not that wild animals would not do, but because with no other creature could he watch a man being torn to pieces utterly and instantaneously.
>
> (Pliny the Elder, *Natural History*, IX. 39)

The poet Martial, by his own account, laid into his cook if a meal was not up to scratch:

> You think me barbaric, Rusticus, and too fond of my food, because I beat my cook when my dinner is below standard.

If that seems to you a trivial reason for the lash, what other excuse is there to flog a cook?

(*Epigrams*, VIII. 23)

Was it ambivalence that inspired another poem? 'You say your hare is not cooked and call for the whip. You'd rather cut up your cook, Rufus, than your hare?' (*Epigrams*, III. 94)

Pliny the Younger used to invite the better-educated members of his staff to join him after dinner for conversation, and remarked of his villa at Laurentum that most of the rooms in the wing which housed his slaves were also perfectly suitable for putting up guests. This kind of sentiment is echoed by Seneca:

> Remember that he whom you call your slave came into life by the same route as you, basks in the same sky, and breathes, lives, and dies in the same way as you do. You can observe the free man in him just as he can see the slave in you. In the proscriptions of Marius many high-born men, on the military ladder to a seat in the senate, were reduced by fate to being shepherds or janitors. You look down at your peril on someone in whose place you could come to be even while you look down on him. I don't want to get too involved in the broader issues of the treatment of slaves, to whom in general we are extremely arrogant, cruel, and abusive. This, however, is the sum of my advice: treat your inferiors as you would want to be treated by your masters.
>
> (*Epistles*, XLVII)

The contrary view is illustrated by an incident shortly before Seneca's enforced death and during the lifetime of Tacitus, who describes it:

> [In AD 61] the city prefect, Pedanius Secundus, was killed by one of his own slaves; the murderer had either been refused his freedom after the price had been agreed, or had fallen in love with a youth and could not bear to have his master as a rival. Whatever the reason, when the time came to take out to execution all the slaves of the household, as was the time-honoured tradition, there was almost a revolution as the people, bent on sparing innocent lives, got together and besieged the senate. In the senate-house itself there were those who protested that the punishment was unfair, though

the majority saw no reason why the law should not be observed.

(*Annals*, XIV. 42)

Among the latter was the jurist, Gaius Cassius, who made an impassioned speech upholding the status quo.

While no one dared speak openly against Cassius, his words were greeted by a confusion of voices expressing pity at the number of victims involved [said to be 400], their ages, sex, and the fact that most of them were indubitably innocent of any crime. In spite of that, the pro-hanging lobby prevailed. The decision could not be put into effect as an enormous crowd gathered, armed with stones and flaming missiles. Nero issued an edict reprimanding the public, and gave orders that the entire route along which the condemned slaves were being led to execution should be lined with soldiers. Cingonius Varro had proposed additionally that the freedmen who had been in the house at the time should be deported. This was vetoed by the emperor on the grounds that an ancient custom, which had withstood pleas of mercy, should not be stretched to incorporate the exercise of unreasonable cruelty.

(*Annals*, XIV. 45)

A slave could purchase his freedom or achieve it by a process of manumission which was at the discretion of the owner, but which became such a popular practice at the beginning of the empire that Augustus introduced laws restricting it. A freedman had full rights of citizenship except that of holding public office. Some freedmen became even richer than the masters they had once served.

EDUCATION

At the beginning of the republic, education was left entirely to the parents, and consisted of a mixture of martial and practical arts. Boys were expected to emulate their fathers, and girls their mothers. From about 250 BC, largely as a result of the influx of educated Greek slaves, tutors were employed in richer homes or were set up as teachers of informal schools. Towards the end of the republic, a two-tier educational system evolved, leading to higher education in oratory and philosophy. At about the age of 7, children of the privileged classes were sent to a primary school (often presided over by a single teacher), where from dawn to the middle of the afternoon, with a break for lunch at home, they learned reading, writing, and arithmetic. Girls as well as boys could benefit from this basic schooling, which seems often to have been in premises designed as shops, with an open front on the street. Pupils sat on wooden benches and wrote out their exercises on tablets which they rested on their knees.

Formal education ceased for girls at the age of 12, but boys who showed academic promise were sent on, if their parents could afford the fees, to 'grammar' school, where they stayed until they assumed the *toga virilis*, pursuing a curriculum which emphasized Greek as well as Latin literature. Much has been made, from allusions in literature and from an often reproduced fresco uncovered at Herculaneum, of the brutality of school-masters. There seems, however, to be no evidence that corporal punishment in Roman times was any more frequent or severe than it was in many schools in Britain well into the twentieth century. And though Horace writes of remembering verses 'dictated to me as a boy by flogger Orbilius' (*Epistles*, II. 1, 70–1), Suetonius describes a man who was less of a disciplinarian:

> Marcus Verrius Flaccus, a freedman, was renowned for his teaching methods. He stimulated his pupils' efforts by competition: setting those at the same level of attainment a subject on which to write and offering a prize for the best essay. This would be a book of antiquarian interest for its beauty or rarity. As a result of his success he was chosen by Augustus to teach his grandsons, and moved into the palace with his whole school on the understanding that he would not take on any more pupils.
>
> (*On Teachers*, XVII)

According to Suetonius in the same book, rhetoric was 'in the early days' taught in schools. By the time of Quintilian towards the end of the first century AD, it had become accepted that rhetoric should be taught in special schools at a higher level, though a pupil might be expected to have had an introduction to the subject before embarking on higher education.

Rhetoric as a subject as well as an art originated in Sicily in the fifth century BC, and was developed in Athens and in Asia

117

Figure 21 Man in a *toga*

Figure 22 Woman in a *palla*

Minor, before becoming an accepted study in Rome. There were basically three branches of oratory: the display of one's art, often in the form of a panegyric or invective (the latter had its counterpart in the medieval Scottish flyting); the persuasion of an audience to a point of view; and the defence or prosecution of a defendant in a court of law. Each of these involved five separate skills: selection of content; arrangement; language; memory; delivery.

While the schools taught traditional religious observances and supplemented the training children received at home in conduct and morality, older boys, as they grew up, were exposed to the influence of the various branches of Greek philosophy, in which the upper classes at least came to find a more acceptable guide to life than in the religion of the state. Leading citizens employed resident philosophers. When Cicero was about 18, he attended lectures in Rome given by Phaedrus the Epicurean; shortly afterwards he listened to Philo of Larissa, head of the Academic school of philosophy, to whose doctrines he remained generally faithful for the rest of his life. When he was 18, Horace studied philosophy in Athens, where in addition to the Academics and the Epicureans he would have come under the influence of the Stoics and the Peripatetics.

DRESS

The Romans applied their ingenuity and use of basic materials and principles not only to solving complicated architectural and engineering problems, but also to their clothes. These had to be simple. Only wool and, to a lesser extent, linen were available, and because needles were of bronze or bone, and thread only of the coarsest quality, stitching or sewing was neither elegant nor particularly effective. Buttons and buttonholes were therefore rarities, and clothes were fastened or held together mainly by enormous safety-pins, belts, or knots, or not at all.

To say that the Romans slept in their underwear is not to suggest, as would be true of many later civilizations, that they did not wash, for bathing was a feature of daily life. It was simply that the time for taking one's bath was in the afternoon. A woman might have a brassière in the form of a band, the purpose of which was to keep the breasts up rather than in. Otherwise, both men and women wore a loin-cloth knotted round the waist, with a belted tunic or shift with short or long sleeves. The male tunic reached to the knees, but women and girls wore one that was longer, sometimes down to the ground. In winter you might wear two tunics, one on top of the other; those particularly susceptible to cold, such as was Augustus, might wear as many as four. For the poorer classes, slaves, and small children, that was the limit of their attire, though Pliny the Elder used to allow his shorthand writer to wear gloves in cold weather so that nothing would reduce the effectiveness with which his thoughts were recorded.

The outer garment, the classic *toga* for men and the *palla* for women, was the standard, and statutory, formal dress for a Roman citizen. It was simply a vast blanket, draped round and over the body, leaving one arm free, and probably held together only by its own weight and its folds, or by faith alone. The *palla* was rectangular in shape. Archaeologists and scholars have concluded, from practical experiments, that the *toga* was in the form of a segment of a circle, along the straight edge of which ran the purple stripe of the *toga praetexta* (worn by boys and also men of senatorial rank), and that it was about $5\frac{1}{2}$ metres long and 2 metres wide at its deepest point. Putting it on, getting the folds to fall correctly, and keeping it adjusted while performing daily tasks, appear to have been almost as much of a problem to the Romans as they have proved to modern scholars, for Suetonius mentions it as a mark of admiration that Vespasian could chat to callers while he was getting dressed. Those who were standing for public office were in the habit of whitening their *toga* with chalk, and were thus known as *candidati* (clothed in glittering white). For dinner-parties, at which the *toga* could have been an intolerable burden, it was often replaced by the *synthesis*, a kind of dressing-gown. Martial is particularly biting about a rich acquaintance who changed his *synthesis* eleven times during a meal.

Cloaks were worn out of doors in bad weather. There was little difference between the footwear of men and women; both usually wore sandals tied round the ankle with thongs, and on more formal occasions the *calceus*, a soft leather shoe.

For men, shaving was the rule between about 100 BC and AD 100, performed with iron razors by a slave or at one of the innumerable barber's shops which were a feature of urban life. Women wore their hair up in a variety of styles varying between the simple, often with a knot or lock at the back falling to the nape, and the intricately curled and over-ornate.

FOOD AND DRINK

The ordinary Roman was not a great eater of meat; the word *frumentum* (corn) also means military food supplies or rations. The army diet, which was carefully supervised, was a balanced one of wheat (which the soldiers themselves ground and made into porridge, bread, or biscuits), some meat (usually bacon), fish, poultry, cheese, vegetables, fruit, salt, olive oil, and raw wine. When there was a delay in getting the corn ration through and meat had to be substituted, the soldiers groused. Officers fared rather better, even in what has been traditionally regarded as the most uncomfortable posting of all, northern Britain. Entries in documents (in the form of thin wooden tablets) relating to the accounts of the commanding officer's household in about AD 100, found since the 1970s at the fort of Vindolanda on Hadrian's Wall, record fresh produce in the form of pork crackling, pork cutlets, pig's trotters, piglet, ham, chicken, venison, anchovies (or other small fish), oysters, eggs, radishes, apples, lentils, beans, pork fat, lard, and butter.

At home, porridge and bread were the staple food of most Romans, many of whom in the city had to rely on the corn dole for their needs.

> Now that state officials are elected by the senate and the people have no votes to sell, they have lost interest. Those who once had a say in the election to power of everyone from consul to legionary commander have taken back seats, claiming as their rights just bread and circuses [i.e. free tokens for corn and free tickets for the games].
>
> (Juvenal, *Satires*, X. 77–81)

In well-to-do homes the regimen was different. *Jentaculum* (breakfast), for those who wanted it, might be bread dipped in wine, or with cheese, dried fruits, or honey. The equivalent of lunch was *prandium*, again a light meal, often consisting of left-overs from the previous day. The main meal of the day, *cena*, was eaten in the middle of the afternoon, after work and the bath, and could, and often did, go on for hours. Dinner-parties were elaborate, and could be dignified or disgusting affairs, depending

121

DAILY LIFE, WORK, AND ENTERTAINMENT

on the discrimination of the host and his choice of guests. Overindulgence was the rule rather than the exception. Cicero wrote to his friend Atticus that when Julius Caesar stopped overnight at his country villa at Pozzuoli (on the coast between Naples and Puteoli) in 45 BC with his retinue (who had to be entertained in three dining-rooms), Caesar 'had a bath at about one . . . oiled his body, and came into dinner. He used an emetic, and so was able to eat and drink to excess, with obvious enjoyment' (*To Atticus*, XIII. 52). Dinner guests reclined on their left elbow at an angle of about 45 degrees to the table, on couches set against three sides of it, and ate with their fingers.

The meal consisted of three parts, within each of which there could be any number of courses served individually or together. *Hors d'œuvre* might be eggs presented in a variety of ways, salads, cooked vegetables, shellfish, snails, and, occasionally, roast stuffed dormice. The main courses illustrate the varieties of meat, game, fish, and fowl that were available, or which were pressed into service in the form of more impressive-sounding dishes: not just beef, lamb, pork, venison, hare, bream, hake, mackerel, mullet, oysters, sole, chicken, duck, goose, and partridge, but also veal, sucking-pig, boar, wild goat, kid, porpoise, crane, flamingo, ostrich, thrush, and turtle-dove. From the only surviving Roman cookery book, we know how all these were sometimes cooked. It is attributed to a noted gourmet of the time of Tiberius called Apicius, who, it is said, having spent nine-tenths of his considerable fortune on good living, which still left him with 10 million sesterces, killed himself. The book is a later compilation, and many of the recipes have been made to work under modern conditions. They reveal that the ambitious host was usually more concerned with exotic ingredients than with exotic tastes – peacock, for instance, features, but only as rissoles. Most main dishes were served in sauce, the basic ingredient of which was a factory-made fish concoction called *liquamen*. The meal would finish with dessert: fruit, cakes, and puddings.

Juvenal provides a hypothetical guest with a simpler country meal: home-grown asparagus and farm eggs as starters; chicken and milk-fed kid for the main course; local pears, oranges, grapes, and apples to finish with. Martial offers his guests in the country, at a dinner-party for seven:

Figure 23 A panel from a mosaic floor (*c.* AD 100) depicting edible fish from the Mediterranean: (clockwise from top left) octopus, spiny lobster, dentex, gilt-headed bream, red mullet, comber (serranus), common bass (bottom right), green wrasse, rainbow wrasse, scorpion fish, moray eel.
(*British Museum*)

Mallow leaves (good for the digestion) . . . lettuce, chopped leeks, mint (for burping), rocket leaves . . . mackerel garnished with rue and sliced egg, and a sow's udder marinated in tuna-fish brine . . . that's the *hors d'œuvre*. For the main course, all served together, tender cuts of lamb, with beans and spring greens, and a chicken and a ham left over from three previous dinners. When you are full, fresh fruit and vintage wine from Nomentum with no dregs.

(*Epigrams*, X. 48, 7–19)

Wine was the national, and natural, drink, usually diluted with water: beer was for Britons and Gauls. Wine was also mixed with honey to make *mulsum*, a cooling aperitif which accompanied the first course at dinner. This was usually made from must, the first treading of the grapes, but Pliny the Elder recommended that dry white wine should be used instead. For those modern readers inclined to try, two tablespoonfuls of honey to a bottle of wine have been suggested. The best wine-producing region in Italy was around the border between Latium and Campania, from which came the excellent Caecuban, Setian, Falernian, and Massic vintages.

HOLIDAYS AND THE GAMES

Not only was the official Roman working day a short one by modern standards, but there were comparatively few working days in the year, except for slaves, who in any case were not allowed to attend public entertainments as spectators. In the reign of Claudius, 159 days in the year were designated public holidays, on 93 of which shows were offered at public expense: in the middle of the fifth century AD, there were 200 holidays a year, on 175 of which public games were held. Originally these games had religious significance, but under the republic more and more secular games were introduced into the calendar

Figure 24 In republican times, after about 175 BC, it was usual for each of the three men appointed to cast the state's bronze, silver, and gold coins respectively to put their names on them (a practice which survives, for instance, on British and American bank notes). This particular design is a token of the promise of the moneyer (T. Didius) to mount a public gladiatorial games if he is elected curule aedile. (Silver *denarius* of 113/ 112 BC, ×2)

ostensibly to celebrate notable events, some of which lasted as long as a fortnight. There were two kinds of games: *ludi scaenici*, or theatrical events, and *ludi circenses*. That the *ludi scaenici* suffered overwhelming competition from the other forms of spectacle is attested to by the much smaller numbers that the stage theatres seated, by the fewer days allocated to them, and by the evidence of the playwright Terence (185–159 BC). A revival of his comedy *The Mother-in-Law* was staged as a part of the funeral games for Lucius Aemilius Paulus in 160 BC. All was going well during the first act, Terence says in a prologue to a further performance that year, when someone announced that the gladiatorial show was about to begin. The audience did not so much melt away as surge out.

Ludi circenses took place in the custom-built circuses, or race-tracks, and amphitheatres. In these days of live, and televised, sporting mass-entertainments – motor-racing, horse-racing, physical team games such as soccer and rugby football, and now even cricket played between teams wearing coloured track suits

it is not difficult to appreciate the Romans' passion for chariot-racing. One can understand, too, their devotion to the particular team they supported, and its colours of white, green, red, or blue, though not necessarily condone the violence that often ensued between gangs of rival supporters. The public adulated the most successful drivers, and there was heavy on-course and off-course betting. The drivers were slaves, but they were also professional sportsmen, who could earn vast sums from winning. The chariots themselves were deliberately constructed to be as light as possible, and were drawn by two, four, or even more horses; the higher the number, the greater was the skill required of the driver, and the more sensational were the crashes and pile-ups. A race was usually seven laps of the track – a total of about 4,000 metres in the Circus Maximus in Rome – with a hair-raising 180 degrees turn at each end of the *spina*, the narrow wall that divided the arena. Though the start was staggered, there were no lanes and apparently no rules, yet during the first and second centuries AD several star charioteers notched up over 1,000 wins each, and there are records of individual horses being in a winning team several hundred times. Gaius Appuleius Diocles, who died at the age of 42, having driven four-horse chariots for twenty-four years, had 1,462 wins in 4,257 starts, and was placed 1,437 times. In the reign of Augustus there might be ten or twelve races in a day: during and after the time of Caligula, twenty-four a day was commonplace.

It was the *ludi circenses* of the amphitheatres, however, which have given the Romans the bad press that their thirst for blood-letting has earned them, though there is evidence that the Etruscans attached religious significance to the gladiatorial combat. The single rule of such bouts was that similarly armed contestants or teams of contestants did not normally fight each other. The most usual contest was between a moderately pro-tected and helmeted swordsman and a *retiarius*, armed only with a net and a trident, or between teams of these. It was each man for himself, and any who appeared less than enthusiastic were prodded into activity with red-hot irons, while other attendants stood by to drag off the corpses. It was sometimes left to the crowd to signify whether a wounded and downed gladiator should be finished off by his opponent. They did so by waving their handkerchiefs for a release, or giving the 'thumbs down' signal for death. Gladiators were slaves, or condemned crim-inals, or prisoners of war, all of whom were regarded as expend-able. So were wild animals, which were rounded up in their natural habitats and transported in their thousands to be hunted down and slaughtered in the confines of the arenas of the Roman empire, as a sickening morning's overture to the gladiatorial contests in the afternoon. To celebrate the opening of the Colosseum in AD 80, 5,000 wild beasts and 4,000 tame animals were killed in one day. For variety, animals would be goaded to fight each other. Elephants versus bulls was a feature of a games in 79 BC. Nero introduced a novel turn, the marine contest: 'Fights between wild animals of the forests are less interesting, now that we have seen seals against bears' (Calpurnius, *Eclogues*, VII, 64–5). Alternatively, or as an additional attraction, the animals tore apart contingents of condemned and unarmed criminals: Christians were regarded as especially good sport.

The third and most spectacular form of combat, which involved flooding the arena or transferring the show to a suita-ble stretch of water, was the *naumachia*, or sea-fight. The idea seems to have originated with Julius Caesar, an impresario of great ingenuity and ambition, who had an artificial lake dug, on which he pitted against each other two fleets of 10,000 oarsmen, with 1,000 soldiers dressed up to represent men of Tyre and Egypt. Particularly popular in later years was a reconstruction of the battle of Salamis in 480 BC, which was replayed several times during the first century AD. The biggest *naumachia* ever was staged by Claudius in AD 52.

> The tunnel through the mountain to drain the Fucine lake into the river Liris had now been completed. [Brick-lined, and 5,600 metres long, it had taken 30,000 workmen eleven years to construct.] In order that as many people as possible might admire the impressiveness of the achievement, a naval battle was arranged on the lake itself. . . . Claudius put 19,000 armed combatants into two fleets of ships with both three and four banks of oars. He positioned rafts round the edge of the lake to block off any escape routes, leaving enough space in the middle for the display of the power of the oarsmen, the skill of the coxes, the speed of the ships, and all the other arts of such a contest. Platoons and companies of the praetorian cohorts were stationed on the rafts, protected by ramparts, from behind which they fired catapults and missile-throwers. Covered ships manned by marines occupied the rest of the lake. . . . The battle, though contested by criminals, was fought as bravely and spiritedly as if the combatants were men of free will, and after considerable bloodshed they were excused death.
>
> (Tacitus, *Annals*, XII. 56)

Hazards were not always confined to the arena itself. When the Circus Maximus was still used for gladiatorial contests, Pompey put up iron barriers to protect the audience during a fight between twenty crazed elephants and bands of armed hunters. The barriers buckled and some of them broke. And in AD 27, a jerry-built amphitheatre at Fidenae collapsed, throwing 50,000 spectators (according to Tacitus, 20,000 according to Suetonius) to the ground and burying them in debris. A redeeming feature of the disaster was the way in which emergency services were provided by the rich, who drafted in medical supplies and doctors from their own households. The response of the government was to issue guidelines for such entertainments: 'No-one with a capital of less than 400,000 sesterces may present a gladiatorial show, and an amphitheatre may only be built on solid ground' (Tacitus, *Annals*, IV. 63).

6

ART, ARCHITECTURE, AND BUILDING

The overriding impression the material arts of Rome offer is of opulence, solid permanence, and the application of practical skills which were largely inherited but which were adapted to the economic and expansionist tendencies that resulted in the growth of the empire. Roman sculpture, learned from the Greeks and Etruscans, reached a peak in the first and second centuries AD which has hardly been matched since. It was, however, the development of the arch, the vault, and the dome, and the use of concrete, which gave distinction, serviceability, and grandeur to Roman domestic and public architecture and civil engineering.

SCULPTURE

Two influences in particular drove the Romans fully to explore and develop the art of sculpture: the worship and reverence of images, not only of gods and goddesses, but also of dead ancestors; and the recording of ritualistic and triumphant events in bas-relief on pillars, arches, and tombs. Whereas the faces of Greek portrait sculptures tend to display neither expression nor emotion, those carved particularly in the time of the Flavian emperors and after have character and animation, often down to the glint of an eye, a technique achieved by using a drill to indicate the ring of the iris and the reflection of light on the pupil. Reality before flattery was demonstrably the rule rather than the exception. No less effective are some of the portraits on coins of the later republic and early empire.

Typical among outstanding historical reliefs are those on the column of the emperor Trajan, erected during his lifetime in AD

113 in the forum which bears his name, to celebrate his conquest, and acquisition for the empire, of Dacia, which equates to present-day Romania. The style of this monument has been imitated several times since: most immediately in the column of Marcus Aurelius, begun in AD 180 and completed in AD 192, recording his victories against the German tribes along the Danube with emphasis on the agony and suffering of the enemy, and most recently by Napoleon in the Place Vendôme in Paris to celebrate his defeats of the Russians and Austrians. Trajan's column is 30 metres high, with a staircase inside lit by forty-three slit windows. A spiral band about 1 metre deep and 200 metres long winds twenty-three times round the shaft from bottom to top, carrying 155 continuous scenes. Though there is not a great deal of attention given to perspective, the effect is of activity and action in which more than 2,500 different human figures have been counted.

The story of Trajan's campaign is built up stage by stage, from the commissioning of the army, its march and crossing of the Danube by a bridge specially built for the purpose, through preparations for the fighting, siege, and battle, to the grim aftermath of the torture of Roman prisoners of war and the suicide of the Dacian chief. Trajan himself appears frequently, at the head of his troops, addressing them before battle, briefing his officers, conducting the ritual sacrifice. The bridge over the fast-moving river took a year to construct, and its architect, Apollodorus of Damascus, also designed Trajan's column; it is not only a monument to the artistic skill of the men who decorated it, but the fullest pictorial source we have of the conduct, uniforms, and arms of the imperial army.

PAINTING AND MOSAIC

As far as we know, paintings were used almost exclusively to cover walls of rooms in houses. These frescoes, of which many are splendidly preserved at Herculaneum and Pompeii, are brightly coloured, and most frequently depict scenes from Greek mythology. Landscapes were employed to give the impression of picture windows – Nero's Golden Palace even has some enclosed in window frames also painted on to the wall – while the effect of a garden was often extended and enhanced by landscape frescoes along its boundary walls. We have still-life

paintings, too, of dead game birds, fish, and vegetables, which may be intended to represent the kinds of gifts which guests would take away from a party.

The art of mosaic seems to have originated in Babylon; it was widely practised in Egypt under the Ptolemies in the third century BC. Because a mosaic is comparatively indestructible and the medium spread throughout the Roman empire to its very outposts, it has come to represent Roman pictorial art to many who have never seen the sculptures and paintings which Italy has to show, and which are not viewed to their best advantage in museum surroundings.

Mosaics were of three kinds. *Opus sectile* consists of small pieces of different-coloured marble cut into various shapes and fitted together in a geometrical pattern which sometimes incorporates floral devices and other emblems. In *opus tessellatum*, the dice are square and all of the same size. The most complex form is *opus vermiculatum*, where the dice are of varied shape and size, often of minute proportions, and have rounded edges. Sometimes more complicated works were made in a studio, and transferred to the site and embedded in concrete, either as wall decorations or pavements. These might be scenes from legend or daily life, or even portraits.

GEM ENGRAVING

Romans were great accumulators of wealth rather than collectors of art, but some of their acquisitions were put to good and artistic use. It was said that Pompey started the craze by his capture of the gem collection of Mithridates, which he put on public display in the temple of Jupiter on the Capitoline Hill. Carved signet rings were widely employed to authenticate legal documents, and the wearing of a ring to denote office or status was an old custom. In the later empire, free-born men wore gold rings, freedmen silver, and slaves iron. Though the Egyptians

← *Figure 25* Scenes from Trajan's Column. In the band below, legionaries are building a fortification. In the foreground above, (left) a medical orderly in a field dressing station patches up a leg-wound, and (centre) a Dacian prisoner is brought before the emperor. Behind (left to right) standards are borne into battle; two musicians carry their *cornua*, circular trumpets used in battle to give orders; carts, driven by mules, transport supplies on the march. (*Deutsches Archaeologisches Institut, Rome*) and the Greeks had used the art of gem engraving, it was brought to a high pitch in Roman times to produce the most delicate portraits. These were cut either in intaglio, by incising the surface of the stone, or cameo, where the figure is made to stand out by carving away the background, a method which can be doubly effective if the stone has layers of different colours, as has onyx or sardonyx.

DOMESTIC ARCHITECTURE

The early Roman town house was little more than a single room known as the *atrium*. The roof sloped inwards and downwards to a rectangular opening, beneath which was a basin, the *impluvium*, set into the floor to catch the rainwater. As time went on, small extra rooms were built inside the *atrium* against its walls, or separated off by partitions. In about the second century BC, the Greek influence began to be felt. The *atrium* with its *impluvium* and the little rooms remained, but now opened into a larger extension, the *peristylum*, a garden court (sometimes with a fountain in the middle) surrounded by a colonnaded passage off which were further rooms. Between the *atrium* and the *peristylum*, and opening into both, was the *tablinum*, which had various uses: a dining-room, especially in summer when it would

Figure 26 Plan of a Roman house
A *vestibulum*   B *atrium*   C *impluvium*   D *tablinum*   E *peristylum*

132

be the coolest place in the house, a reception room, or an office for the head of the household.

The main doors into the house from the outside were usually set back from the street and approached through the *vestibulum*. Such a house would be unlikely to consist of more than one storey, though upstairs dining-rooms are sometimes referred to by writers of the times. Apartments above shops, however, reached by an outside staircase, were a feature of small towns. Urban congestion was a problem in Rome from early times. It has been estimated from statistics compiled at the time that in the second century AD there were 1,782 houses in the city, providing accommodation for 50,000 people, many of whom would have been household slaves. The other 1.5 million lived, as the majority do in Rome today, in tenement blocks, six or even seven storeys high. Augustus limited their height to 20 metres: Trajan lowered this to 18. Many of them were cheaply built on unsound foundations. Collapsed blocks were commonplace, rent irregularities were rife, and sanitation was superficial. Comparatively well-to-do flat dwellers lived on the ground floor and had access to a public sewer. Even in the purpose-built new-town apartment blocks in Ostia, it would appear that upstairs private latrines were not connected to any public sewer. Upper-floor tenants in Rome had to make their own arrangements, though there were public lavatories for those who could afford them. The rest had recourse to chamber pots, the contents of which they emptied into a well at the foot of the stairs, or threw out of the window into the street below, a practice still prevailing in eighteenth-century Edinburgh, which had a similar population problem.

For the rich, there were two kinds of villa, or country house. The *villa rustica* was a glorified farmhouse which contained living-quarters for the owner of the estate when he happened to be in residence. The *villa urbana* was where you luxuriated or retreated for a holiday from the bustle of Rome, or stopped off for a night on a journey, or even stayed after a hard day's work in the city. Cicero, who was by no means one of the richest men of his time, owned seven houses in the country, each of which he used from time to time. Pliny the Younger, who *was* very rich, had at least four, including one in Etruria where he spent the summer, and an especially opulent one on the seashore at Laurentum, where he lived in the winter, but which was near

Figure 27 Public latrines, such as this one in Ostia, also served a social function. 'Vacerra haunts the public loos, where he sits all day – not shitting, just cadging a meal' (Martial, *Epigrams*, XI. 77). The trend extended to private houses: the villa at Settefinestre, near Cosa, built in 75 BC, sports a communal lavatory seating twenty people at a time. (*C. M. Dixon*)

enough to Rome, with a good road between, for him to be able to ride home after a full day's business in the city.

In the villa, the principal parts of the town house were usually reversed, the entrance opening into the *peristylum*, behind which was the *atrium*. Plans of houses that have been excavated can tell us about the shape, size, and probable use to which the various rooms were put. In a letter to his friend Gallus, Pliny describes in detail what many of the rooms in his winter villa looked like, and for what they were used. Apart from the usual features, it had two towers, with bedrooms commanding magnificent views, a series of sitting-rooms, several studies (one of which had built-in bookcases and got the sun all day through a bay window), a centrally heated bedroom, an outdoor gymnasium for the staff, a ball court, and a swimming pool. Some if not all of the windows were glazed. The only drawback, according to Pliny, was that there was no running water, but he adds that there were three public baths in the nearby village if for any reason it was inconvenient to heat up the water at home. Central heating was invented by Sergius Oresta in about 100 BC, and was achieved by circulating hot air from a furnace through cavities under the floor and inside the walls. Not unnaturally, it is a particular feature of villas found in Britain.

THE ARCHITECTURE OF PUBLIC BUILDINGS

The Romans did not invent the arch, but their development of it enabled them fully to exploit their penchant for massive constructions and for resolving improbable situations by vast expense of labour. From the Greeks they took the three orders of architecture, Doric, Ionic, and Corinthian, based on different forms of column and the capital which surmounted it, and added to them a hybrid of their own, known as Composite. It was, however, a mark of eccentric extravagance to decorate the façades of public buildings, especially theatres and amphitheatres, with rows of columns in tiers, and to use a different order for each. That they could indulge their architectural ambitions was due also to the indubitably Roman invention of concrete. Its basis was *pozzolana*, a chocolate-coloured volcanic earth originally found near the Greek settlement of Puteoli, which when mixed with lime formed a powerful, waterproof cement. It was then discovered that vast quantities of *pozzolana* could be quarried around Rome. It was used to make mortar and also, when mixed with lime and strengthening materials such as chips of rock and broken brick, concrete. Judicious use of bricks and concrete together enabled massive, permanent structures to be built.

Their command of materials and techniques enabled the Romans to construct circular temples, perhaps consciously imitating the round huts of the original Italians, as in the quaint, shallow-roofed temple, now the Church of Santa Maria del Sol, only 8 metres in diameter and surrounded by twenty columns, which was built in the first century BC. The most spectacular example is the Pantheon, crowned by a hemispherical dome, 43.28 metres in diameter, which if completed would exactly touch the ground. The only light falls through a circular hole, eight metres wide, in the top of the dome. The present building was constructed between AD 120 and 124 in the reign of the emperor Hadrian.

The remains of Roman buildings are a guide to the enormous

areas which some of them covered. The Basilica Julia in the forum of Rome, a colonnaded hall designed primarily as a court of law, measured 100 by 36 metres. The main block of the baths of Caracalla, just outside the Appian gate to the south-east of the city, which could accommodate 1,600 bathers at a time, was 216 by 112 metres. Reconstructions of parts of ancient Rome in model form give some idea of the haphazard siting and comparative size of public buildings, and of the triumphal arches, columns, and statues crammed into this extraordinary urban complex. Neither remains nor reconstructions, however, can reliably reflect the sheer height of so many of them or the inspiration which governed their design. Roman architects were less concerned with external appearances than with the creation of interior space. This can still be experienced in the Pantheon and in the Church of Santa Maria degli Angeli in Rome, converted by Michelangelo in 1563 from just one hall of the baths of Diocletian, completed in about AD 305 and capable of accommodating twice the number of customers as the baths of Caracalla. The dome, where it was employed, enhanced the impression of vastness. From constructing it on a circular base, the architects progressed to domed buildings on a polygonal plan. And in their construction of public baths as palaces of luxury-cum-cultural, leisure, and sports centres, the Romans combined their passion for opulence with their flair for hydraulics. The essential rooms, separate for men and women, were the centrally heated *tepidarium,* where bathers were encouraged to sweat after removing their clothes; the *caldarium,* where they bathed in tubs of hot water; and the *frigidarium,* where they took a cold plunge. The water was heated by furnaces and circulated by means of cisterns and pipes.

← *Figure 28* Model of imperial Rome in the Museo della Civiltà Romana: a view from the south. The river Tiber is on the left, and beyond it (centre, far left) the Temple of Jupiter stands on the Capitoline Hill. The Circus Maximus is in the foreground; behind it, on the Palatine Hill, is the imperial palace complex, from which the Claudian aqueduct snakes out. The larger columned building to the north of the palace is the Temple of Venus and Roma, to the west of which are the Basilica of Constantine, the Temple of Peace, and the Basilica Aemilia, which fronts on to the east end of the forum. To the north-east of the palace is the Colosseum, behind which are the baths of Trajan. The large building to the south-east of the Colosseum is the Temple of Claudius. (*C.M. Dixon*)

For their theatres, the Romans followed the Greek plan of tiers of seats in a semi-circle facing the stage, but whereas the Greeks tended to take advantage of natural slopes on which to erect the seats, Roman theatres were usually built on level ground. Some of the smaller ones were covered, thus also improving the acoustics and making them particularly suitable for musical performances. The first stone theatre in Rome was opened in 55 BC, and by 13 BC there were two more. The smallest of these could seat 7,500 and the largest 14,000, compared with the 3,000 capacity of the present Scala in Milan, the 2,200 of the Royal Opera House in London, and the 3,800 of the former Metropolitan Opera House in New York. These figures are minute, however, beside the Colosseum and the 635-metre-long Circus Maximus, where 265,000 spectators at a time watched the chariot races.

The Romans took their architectural techniques with them, wherever they settled. When they left Britain in about AD 400, it was to the marauding and looting of waves of Saxons and Danes. Even these, however, and further centuries of violent unrest, have not entirely obliterated the skeletons of an amphitheatre in Chester, a public baths in Bath, and a theatre, capable of seating 6,000, in St Albans; while traces of a huge basilica, 150 metres long, have been discovered under offices in the City of London, and ruins nearby of a second-century AD temple of Mithras. Even more solid evidence of the Romanization of their extensive empire stands in parts of North Africa and the Near East, and in what was the province of Gaul. Julius Caesar made Lutetia Parisiorum (Lutetia, tribal capital of the Parisii) a centre of provincial administration, and Paris has revealed Roman origins for some of its streets, traces of a forum, and remains of three public baths and an amphitheatre. Trier, on the Moselle, became even more important during Roman times than Paris, and contains substantial portions of public buildings and a completely restored audience-hall. The biggest cluster of remains outside Italy is in Provence, where Arles, Nîmes, and Orange can between them boast two amphitheatres, two theatres, a temple, and a triumphal arch.

The extension and retention of an empire required the construction of town walls to discourage attackers, and in the case of Hadrian's Wall in Britain to keep a whole invasion force at bay. Roads and bridges were needed for speedy communications and

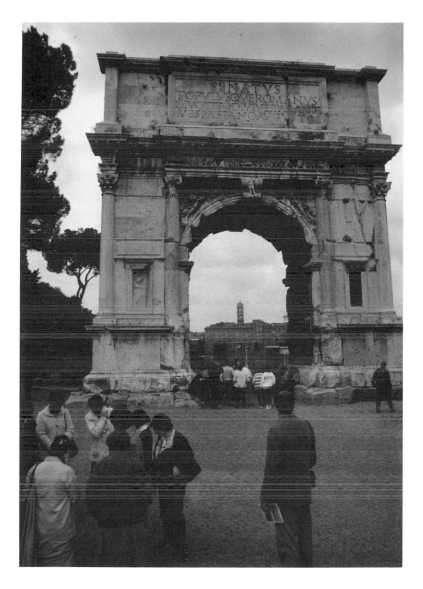

Figure 29   The Arch of Titus, 15 metres high and 12 wide, was, according to its inscription, erected by the senate and the Roman people (often abbreviated to SPQR) to commemorate the deified Titus. It particularly celebrates his exploits in the war against the Jews. A triumphal arch had a special significance: it reflected the triumph voted by the senate to a successful military commander. (*Richard Stoneman*)

the deployment of troops, and aqueducts to supply populations adequately with water. Towns on exposed ground could comparatively quickly be turned into fortresses by the raising of walls consisting of a base of large stone blocks, then a deep course of rubble faced with concrete, topped off with alternate layers of stone and tiles. More permanent defences called for an elaborate standard procedure which involved digging ditches 30 Roman feet deep and 100 feet wide – a Roman foot was 29.59 centimetres. The earth that had been excavated was built up into a mound behind the ditch and supported on either side by a retaining wall of standard-sized blocks of tufa rock: the end result was about 15 metres deep and 15 metres high. Hadrian's Wall was built between AD 122 and 127 on the orders of the emperor Hadrian, and supervised by his friend and governor of Britain, Aulus Platorius Nepos. Its purpose was to

Figure 30 Hadrian's Wall ran 117 km from coast to coast, following the natural crags in the terrain. It comprised a V-shaped ditch up to 5 metres deep and 12 wide, dug where necessary out of solid rock: behind it was a wall 5 metres high and about 3 metres wide, with battlements on top.
There were seventeen forts along its length; in addition a tower was erected at every Roman mile (1,000 *passus*: 1 *passus* = 5 Roman feet = 1.48 m). Between each pair of towers were two fortified turrets. (*Richard Stoneman*)

keep in their native northern parts the tribes who had been defeated by Agricola at Mons Graupius, near Aberdeen, in AD 84, but who had subsequently been allowed to regroup unmolested.

The empire was kept together by a network of roads, branching out from all the main towns and joining up with the quickest and safest sea routes. The building and upkeep of roads were the responsibility of the state, and military roads in the provinces were constructed by the army, with some additional forced labour from the local people. According to an 'itinerary' compiled in the reign of Antoninus (AD 138–61), the extent of metalled or paved roads in Italy was approximately 22,400 km; in Gaul 14,000 km; in Spain 11,200 km; in Britain (parts of which were still unknown) 4,500 km; in Africa 14,000 km; in Asia 15,200 km. All were provided with milestones – there were 5 Roman feet to a *passus* (pace) and 1,000 paces to a Roman mile (*mille passus* or *mille passuum*), which was thus 1.48 km. In AD 68, a special messenger reached Clunia, in northern Spain, from Rome (2,000 km) in 6½ days; the following year another messenger travelled from Mainz via Rheims to Rome (2,100 km) in nine days.

A solitary triumphal arch can hardly give aesthetic satisfaction unless its proportions are in tune with its surroundings, and it is unlikely that the ancient designers of these extraordinary structures thought much about that aspect. Thus to succeeding generations the true triumphal arches of Rome are those which support the bridges which have survived, all the more impressive in that it was not always possible to employ the ingenious course of diverting the river temporarily while the bridge was being built. Early bridges were made of wood, as in later times were military bridges, which could then be destroyed to prevent them being used by the enemy. When Augustus had the roads of Italy renovated, he also built new bridges, of which the ornate, low, five-arched one at Rimini is still in use. So, in very much its original form, is the much longer and earlier Milvian Bridge in Rome, constructed in 109 BC of unmortared blocks of tufa and limestone. At Alcantara in Spain, six arches of unmortared granite blocks, the two centre ones 55 metres above the water, carry the road across the river Tagus. The bridge was built in about AD 106, and an inscription in a temple nearby reads: 'The

141

Figure 31 The Pont du Gard, 25 km west of Avignon, carried water along a channel on top of three tiers of enormous arches which tower 50 metres above the river. (*James Bromwich*)

celebrated Lacer built this bridge with supreme skill to endure through the ages to eternity.' He did and it still does.

The arch enables wide spaces to be crossed by the use of the minimum of materials, thus relieving weight which would otherwise put an intolerable burden on the structure. To the countryman, the most astonishing manifestation of the civilization of Rome must have been the rows of arches, sometimes three tiers of them, which marched across the plains, bringing fresh water from the mountain springs and lakes in a covered channel gently down in an imperceptible gradient into the intricate mechanism which piped it through the towns. The Romans knew all about the rule of dynamics that water always rises to the level of its source. They did use underground pipes, and where necessary tunnelled through hills which could easily be skirted, but building materials and labour were cheap and readily available, whereas large-bore pipes were expensive and less reliable.

The most notable survivor of these monster creations is the Pont du Gard, where it crosses the river near Nîmes. The most famous in ancient times was the Claudian aqueduct, begun by Caligula and finished by Claudius, which had a channel 70 km long and which started its final overhead descent to Rome 12 km out. This was just one of a total of eleven similar structures which brought water to the city. The municipal water board which maintained the system consisted of 460 slaves whom Claudius had taken on to his personal staff, with a special commissioner, a freedman, in charge. In AD 97 Nerva appointed as inspector of aqueducts Sextus Julius Frontinus (AD *c.* 40–103), a former governor of Britain. In his exhaustive report on the system, he estimated that over 1,000 million litres of water a day came into Rome through the eight aqueducts which were then operational.

7

LATIN LITERATURE

Three of the many dialects of the ancient speech which wandering immigrants first brought to the Italian peninsula emerged as contenders for the ultimate language of the region: Umbrian, Oscan, and Latin. Latin, which was used in the comparatively small area of Latium, had been enriched by an admixture of features of local Sabine and Etruscan speech, and much more significantly by Greek. The historical Trojan War took place in about 1220 BC, and legend has it that soon afterwards Greek settlers came to Italy. Certainly there was a Greek trading post in the Bay of Naples by 775 BC, and the fifty years or so after the traditional date for the founding of Rome in 753 BC coincide with the composition of the Greek epic poems, the *Odyssey* and *Iliad*, and the establishment and circulation through the Greek world of the Greek alphabet. The domination of one dialect over another is usually due to external rather than linguistic features – the south-eastern dialect of English became the standard form because London, where it was spoken, was the centre of government and where the English printing industry began. In the case of Latin, it was Roman military expansion which caused it to become the first language of the Italian peninsula and the second, if not the first, wherever else Rome's conquests lay.

From the Latin alphabet is derived the English alphabet, and to all intents and purposes they are the same. Since no one knows exactly how Latin was pronounced – there are at least two 'standard' pronunciations taught – anyone without any knowledge of Latin who reads it aloud cannot go very far wrong. This is important, because whereas the flowering of English literature, for instance, occurred after the introduction of printing, much of Latin literature was expressly written to be read or spoken aloud.

Not that the Romans were without books. The Latin word *liber*, originally the inner part of the bark of a tree which even more ancient Italians had used as a writing surface, meant to the Romans anything that was written. The equivalent of our 'book' was *volumen* (volume), meaning 'roll'. This literally was a roll of papyrus up to 10 metres long and 30 centimetres deep, with a rod fixed at each end, on which the work was written in columns about 10 centimetres wide. To read a book, rolling up the used portion with the left hand while unrolling the rest with the right, required both dexterity and strength, though reading desks were supplied in libraries. The word 'library' also comes from *liber*. Julius Caesar had the idea of opening a public library, but the project lapsed on his death; the credit for founding the first one in Rome goes to Asinius Pollio (76 BC–AD 4). Publishers employed teams of educated slaves to do the copying, and booksellers advertised and sold the results. Importunate acquaintances were an occupational hazard for authors, in precisely the same way as they can be today.

> Whenever we meet, Lupercus, you immediately say: 'May I send my boy to pick up a copy of your new book? I'll give it back as soon as I've read it.' Lupercus, don't bother the boy: it's a long way to my district, and I live up three flights of stairs, long ones, too. You'll find what you want much nearer. I guess you're often in the Argus shopping precinct. Opposite the forum of Caesar there's a bookshop whose front is covered with advertisements: you can see at a glance which poets are available. Ask for Atrectus – he's the owner – and he'll get down for you from the first or second shelf a Martial, smoothed with pumice-stone and bound in purple, for 5 *denarii*. 'You're not worth that,' I hear you say? You're a sensible chap, Lupercus!
>
> (Martial, *Epigrams*, I. 117)

The most striking feature of Latin is its use of inflections, that is changes in the form of a word to indicate, for example, gender, number, case, person, degree, voice, mood, or tense. The order of words in a sentence was flexible and could be varied for the sake of emphasis, different minutiae of meaning, or simply rhythm. Alliteration was widely used in both verse and prose,

145

but rhyme only rarely, and then usually internally in prose. Poetry was written in prescribed metre patterns, made up of short and long syllables, arranged in 'feet', as in Shakespeare's line:

⌣ __1__ ⌣ __2__ ⌣ 3 __ ⌣ 4 __ ⌣ 5 __

Uneas|y lies|the head|that wears|a crown

This is the classic iambic pentameter of five feet, each comprising one short and one long syllable, which is the basis of all the verse in Shakespeare's plays. The equivalent line in Latin poetry is the dactylic hexameter (borrowed from Greek) of six feet, each of one long and two short syllables, or of two long syllables, with a break in the middle of the third foot called a *caesura*.

1 ⌣⌣ 2 ⌣⌣ 3 ⌣⌣ 4 ⌣⌣ 5 6 ⌣

— — | — — | — ‖ — | — — | — ⌣⌣ | — —

Which we can apply to the first line of Virgil's *Aeneid*:

— ⌣1 ⌣ — 2 ⌣ ⌣ — 3 — __4__ __ 5 ⌣ ⌣ __6__

Arma vi|rumque ca|no, ‖ Tro|iae qui|primus ab|oris

(I sing of arms and the man, who first from Trojan shores . . .) Note that in Latin, when the letter 'i' comes before a vowel in the same syllable, as in 'Troiae', it has the effect of the English 'y', as in 'you'. In modern English it is represented by, and sounded as, the letter 'j', as in 'junior' (Latin *iunior*) and 'Julius' (Latin *Iulius*).

In English prosody iambic pentameters rhyming in pairs are known as heroic couplets, a form perfected by John Dryden (1631–1700) and Alexander Pope (1688–1744). The equivalent in Latin is the graceful elegiac couplet: a dactylic hexameter followed by a pentameter, a line of five feet made up of two parts, each of two and a half feet.

— ⌣⌣ — ⌣ ⌣ — ⌣ ⌣ — — — ⌣ — —

Cynthia | prima su|is‖mise|rum me | cepit o|cellis

— ⌣⌣ — — — — ⌣ ⌣ — ⌣ ⌣ —

Contac|tum nul|lis‖ante cu|pidini|bus

(Propertius, *Elegies*, I. 1, 1–2)

146

(Cynthia's dear eyes were the first to ensnare my luckless self, never until then aroused by love's desires.)

Another Greek metre, the hendecasyllable, widely used, especially by Catullus and Martial, comprises eleven syllables:

$$- - -\quad \smallsmile\smallsmile\; -\; \smallsmile\; -\quad \smallsmile\; -\; \smallsmile$$

Vivamus mea Lesbia atque amemus

(Catullus, Poems, V. 1)

(Come, Lesbia, let us live and love . . .) Note that where a word which ends in a vowel precedes one which begins with a vowel, the former vowel is 'elided' or suppressed.

A translation can never totally recapture all aspects of the original, but it can reflect its spirit: the meaning, flavour, and often the flow as well. Translation is a craft of the creative imagination. Just as a translation should be into the first language of the translator, so the translator needs to be a skilled exponent in that language of the medium into which the original is being translated, whether it is prose or verse. The flexibility as well as the precision of Latin were well suited to the verse forms which Roman poets employed, as Alfred Lord Tennyson (1809–92) acknowledged in the case of Virgil, whom he addresses by the Italian epithet of the place of his birth:

> I salute thee, Mantovano,
> I that loved thee since my day began,
> Wielder of the stateliest measure
> Ever moulded by the lips of man.
> (*To Virgil*, 37–40)

Because of the essential differences between the two languages and between the ways in which metrical weight and stress-accent are disposed, the stateliness of Virgil's lines cannot be reflected in English by the use of hexameters. English verse *has* been written in hexameters, notably by Arthur Hugh Clough (1819–61), where the effect is not at all heroic, but intentionally mock-heroic:

It was the afternoon; and the sports were now at the ending.
Long had the stone been put, tree cast, and thrown the
hammer;
Up the perpendicular hill, Sir Hector so called it,
Eight stout gillies had run, with speed and agility wondrous;
Run too the course on the level had been; the leaping was
over.

(The Bothie of Tober-na-Vuolich, I. 1–5)

There have been numerous prose translations of Virgil, and
many also in verse, of which Dryden's, though by no means the
most accurate, gets nearest to the stateliness and possibly to the
spirit, too.

Arms, and the man I sing, who, forc'd by fate,
And haughty Juno's unrelenting hate,
Expell'd and exil'd, left the Trojan shore.
Long labors, both by sea and land, he bore,
And in the doubtful war, before he won
The Latin realm, and built the destin'd town;
His banish'd gods restor'd to rites divine,
And settled sure succession in his line,
From whence the race of Alban fathers come,
And the long glories of majestic Rome.

(Aeneid, I. 1–7, tr. John Dryden)

Not that the hexameter form was rigid in its application.
Virgil used it also for his pastoral and didactic poems, the
Eclogues and *Georgics,* and Juvenal for his *Satires,* brimming with
cameos of city life and of contemporary *mores.* So Dryden, in his
translations of Juvenal, represented the linguistic and narrative
spirit of the original again in the medium of which he was a
master, the heroic couplet: as in the reflections on the hazards of
living in Rome and the tribulations of those who face the nightly
fear of fire.

Codrus had but one bed, so short to boot,
That his short wife's short legs hung dangling out;
His cupboard's head six earthen pitchers grac'd,
Beneath 'em was his trusty tankard plac'd;
And, to support this noble plate, there lay
A bending Chiron cast from honest clay;
His few Greek books a rotten chest contain'd,

148

Whose covers much of moldiness complain'd:
Where mice and rats devour'd poetic bread,
And with heroic verse luxuriously were fed.
'Tis true, poor Codrus nothing had to boast,
And yet poor Codrus all that nothing lost;
Begg'd naked thro' the streets of wealthy Rome;
And found not one to feed, or take him home.

(Satire III. 203–11, tr. John Dryden)

ENNIUS

Quintus Ennius (239–169 BC) is regarded as the father of Latin poetry. He has been referred to as the 'Chaucer of Roman literature', which is misleading in that Chaucer's birthplace was London and early on he had access to the royal court, whereas Ennius was born of Greek parentage in Rudiae in Calabria, the 'heel' of Italy. As well as Greek, however, he spoke Latin and the local Oscan dialect. As a subject of Rome, he served in Sardinia in the Second Punic War. He was still there, presumably as a member of a garrison, in 204 BC, for there he met Cato, then praetor, who took him back to Rome. Ennius lived frugally, writing and earning a living by teaching the sons of the nobility, with whom he was on good terms. He was granted Roman citizenship in 184 BC.

Ennius wrote over twenty stage tragedies, mainly on Greek themes, as well as some comedies and occasional verses. His main work, on which he was engaged for the last twenty years of his life, was a massive verse history of Rome up to his own day (omitting the First Punic War), in eighteen books. For this, he abandoned the rough and barely perceptible rhythms of earlier Latin poets for the stately and musical measures of the hexameter, which he forged into the epic medium later used by Virgil. We have only fragments of Ennius's work totalling some 600 lines, which may not be his best, but he was often quoted by later writers.

COMEDY: PLAUTUS AND TERENCE

The first comic dramas that the Romans saw were based on the Greek 'new comedies' of the kind staged in Athens from about 400 to 200 BC. Their hallmarks included stratagems and

Figure 32 The principal writer of the Greek 'new comedy' was Menander (342– *c.* 292 BC), whose situation comedies influenced Plautus and Terence. This second-century or early first-century BC mosaic from Pompeii illustrates a scene from Menander's play, *Ladies at Lunch*, of which only a few lines survive. (*C. M. Dixon*)

counter-stratagems, stock characters (young lovers, scheming slave, family hanger-on), and standard situations (obstacles to young love, mistaken identities, revelations of true identity), with some musical accompaniment. Titus Maccus Plautus (254–184 BC) was not the first of these Roman dramatists, but of 130 plays attributed to him twenty have survived. This in itself is a measure of popularity, were it not also that in spite of being based on earlier Greek models, his work retains a raw freshness of its own. He worked out ways of adapting Greek verse metres to the Latin language, introduced to audiences whose taste had tended towards farce and slapstick several varieties of literary comedy, such as burlesque and domestic and romantic pieces, in which verbal fireworks replaced crude banter. He also surmounted the problem of playing consecutive scenes, without any breaks between them, in front of a standard back-drop, usually a street with the entrances to two houses.

Plautus was born in Sarsina, a small village in Umbria, but left home early to go to Rome. He seems to have been stage-struck, for he first worked as a props-man and then, with the money he had earned, set himself up in the same kind of business. When that failed, he took a job turning a baker's handmill, which he was able to give up after writing his first three plays. Shakespeare's *Comedy of Errors* is based on Plautus's *The Brothers Menaechmus*; the protagonist of *The Braggart Soldier* of Plautus is the prototype of the Elizabethan stage boaster, whose appearance in *Ralph Roister Doister* by Nicolas Udall (1505–56) marks the beginning of English comedy written for public performance.

Publius Terentius Afer (185–159 BC) was brought to Rome as a slave, possibly from Africa. He took his name from that of his owner, Terentius Lucanus, who educated him and gave him his freedom. The story goes that he submitted his first play, *The Girl from Andros*, to the curule aediles (one of whose functions was to act as municipal entertainments' officers); they referred him to Caecilius Statius (c. 219–c. 166 BC), the most popular playwright of the day. Caecilius was at dinner when Terence called, but immediately began to read the play aloud. He was so impressed by it that he invited Terence to join the dinner guests and to share the couch of honour with him. The play was first performed in 166 BC, and Terence wrote five more before he died in a shipwreck, or of disease, while on a trip to Greece to find further plots. He was only about 26. His plays are better plotted than those of Plautus and of some of the originals which he adapted. With him the comedy of manners effectively began. He was adept at employing the double plot, especially to illustrate different characters' responses to a situation, and in developing the situation itself. There is more purity of language and characterization than in Plautus, which may account for Terence being nothing like as popular in his own day as he was to become later. William Congreve (1670–1729), in a preface to his play *The Way of the World*, extols 'the Purity of [Terence's] Stile, the Delicacy of his Turns, and the Justness of his Characters'; the French philosopher and writer Denis Diderot (1713–84) said that of all writers of comedy only Terence and Molière (1622–73) had the gift of individualizing their characters in a timeless way.

LUCRETIUS

In the dark, confused days presaging the end of the republic, voices were abroad which questioned prevailing views about the natural and spiritual worlds. Some of these belonged to the Epicureans, a school of Greek philosophers founded by Epicurus (341–270 BC) whose tenets included a rudimentary theory of the atomic nature of matter. Epicurus believed, too, that every happening had a natural cause and that the ultimate aim in life was the pleasure that could be derived from the harmony of body and mind. Among the staunchest followers of Epicureanism in Italy was Titus Lucretius Carus (*c.* 99–55 BC), about whom we know nothing else except the story that he was poisoned by an aphrodisiac, went mad, wrote poetry in his lucid spells, and committed suicide at the age of 44.

That Lucretius was mad is unlikely: that his great project ultimately proved too much for him is possible. *De Rerum Natura* (On the Nature of Things) comprises the first six books, some 7,500 hexameters, of an unfinished philosophical poem unique in Latin and with few equivalents in other literatures – the nearest in English is *Testament of Beauty* by Robert Bridges (1844–1930). It is a work of great learning and great poetry; also of considerable insight, in that while subscribing to the Epicurean objection to spiritual gods and their images, he anticipated the kind of dilemma the modern biologist has with regard, for instance, to Christianity. So Lucretius invests Venus, whom he invokes at the beginning of the poem, with an overall creative power in nature, before entering into his exposition of the composition of matter and space in atomic terms, and going on to discuss the mind, life itself, feeling, sex, thought, cosmology, anthropology, meteorology, and geology. *De Rerum Natura* is thus not so much a philosophical work as a scientific treatise; it is a mark of the skill of Lucretius that he succeeded in presenting it in the language and metre of poetry.

LYRIC POETRY: CATULLUS AND HORACE

Lyric poetry has come to mean that in which the composer presents his or her personal thoughts and feelings. Originally, it simply meant poetry or a song accompanied by the lyre, for which the Greek poets used a variety of metres. The Romans took over the metres, though not necessarily the accompaniment, and employed them in a rather more precise form to express themselves poetically.

Gaius Valerius Catullus (*c.* 85–53 BC) was born in Verona, in the north of Italy, probably of a moderately rich family. Certainly, when he arrived in Rome in about 62 BC, it was not to look for a job. He became one of the wave of 'new poets' who reacted against their elders while, from the evidence of his own poetry, boozing, whoring, and generally living it up. Catullus, at any rate, moved in high circles, especially if the woman he calls Lesbia in his poems, and with whom he had a blazing affair, was Clodia, emancipated and profligate sister of Cicero's archenemy Publius Clodius and the wife of Metellus Celer, consul in 60 BC. In this case she would have been rather older than her ill-starred lover. In 57 BC, Catullus was the guest, or camp-follower, of Memmius, governor of Bithynia, to whom Lucretius dedicated *De Rerum Natura*. He died soon after returning to Italy.

In spite of his comparatively early death, Catullus was still not by any means a prolific writer. We have just 116 poems, varying in length from two to 408 lines, and a few brief fragments, which probably represent the whole of his published work. Many of them are bitingly observant cameos of friends and enemies (among the latter was Julius Caesar), of chance meetings and alfresco sexual encounters, in which he is often coarse but always amusing. Others, including his longest (Poem LXIV), an account in hexameters of the wedding of Peleus and Thetis, have mythological themes, but still show depth of poetic emotion. And there are of course the famous love/hate poems to Lesbia/Clodia – passionate, tender, sometimes bitter.

> Sparrow, my Lesbia's darling pet,
> Her playmate whom she loves to let
> Perch in her bosom and then tease
> With tantalising fingertips,
> Provoking angry little nips
> (For my bright beauty seems to get
> A kind of pleasure from these games,
> Even relief, this being her way,
> I think, of damping down the flames
> Of passion), I wish I could play

Silly games with you, too, to ease
My worries and my miseries.
(Poem II, tr. James Michie)

One cannot discount the parallels between Catullus's affair
with Lesbia and Shakespeare's with his 'dark lady' of the sonnets,
and especially between Catullus's denunciation of his mistress as
a whore (Poems 37 and 58) and Shakespeare's of his as 'the bay
where all men ride' (Sonnet 137). Of all English poets, Byron is
probably nearest to Catullus in temperament, habits, and poetic
genius. Byron himself may have recognized this, for while still in
his teens he translated two of the poems (3 and 51) into,
unfortunately, some of his lesser verse.

Whereas Catullus often wrote in the passions of the moment,
his successor, Quintus Horatius Flaccus (65–8 BC), had the leisure
and time to marshal his thoughts into lines which usually display
more grace and artifice than those of Catullus, but less emotion.
Horace was born in Venusia, Apulia, son of a freedman who
made quite a living for himself, and acquired a small estate, by
collecting taxes on sales at agricultural auctions. Instead of going
to the local school, which was attended by sons of the rural
aristocracy, Horace was taken by his father to Rome. There he
was sent to the best educational establishments and was taught
by the formidable pedagogue Orbilius, who was born in 113 BC
and lived to be nearly 100. At 18, Horace went to Athens to
continue his education, but was caught up in the civil war which
followed the assassination of Julius Caesar and fought at Philippi, unfortunately on the wrong side, as a legionary commander in the army of Brutus. He was pardoned for this lapse of
loyalty, but when he got back to Rome he found that his father's
estate had been confiscated. He became a civil service clerk and
in his spare time wrote verses which caught the eye of Virgil,
who introduced him to his own patron, Gaius Maecenas (c. 70–8
BC). A few years later Maecenas set Horace up in a farm near
Tibur at the foot of the mountains to the east of Rome, the
remains of which still survive. Between this farm, a cottage in
Tibur, and a house in Rome, Horace lived out his existence as a
bachelor with, when it suited him, Epicurean tendencies.

Horace's lyric poetry comprises his seventeen Epodes, and 103
Odes in four books. The former, which include some of his early
work, are on a variety of political and satirical themes, with a few

love poems. Most are written in an iambic metre, a longer line being followed by a shorter one, which is known as the 'epode', or 'after song'. The first three books of odes were written between 33 and 23 BC and reflect the events of the time: the opening line of the fourth verse of this one is the celebrated saying, '*dulce et decorum est pro patria mori*':

> Disciplined in the school of hard campaigning,
> Let the young Roman study how to bear
> Rigorous difficulties without complaining,
> And camp with danger in the open air.
>
> And with his horse and lance become the scourge of
> Wild Parthians. From the ramparts of the town
> Of the warring king, the princess on the verge of
> Womanhood with her mother shall look down
>
> And sigh, 'Ah, royal lover, still a stranger
> To battle, do not recklessly excite
> That lion, savage to touch, whom murderous anger
> Drives headlong through the thickest of the fight.'
>
> The glorious and decent way of dying
> Is for one's country. Run, and death will seize
> You no less surely. The young coward, flying,
> Gets his quietus in the back and knees. . . .
>
> (*Odes*, III. 2, 1–16, tr. James Michie)

The fourth book was published in 15 BC. Horace's odes are regarded as his finest works and are written in a variety of Greek metres whose rules he followed strictly. His other works include *Carmen Saeculare*, a poem to various gods, commissioned by Augustus to celebrate the Saecular Games in 17 BC; three books of Epistles, of which the third is generally known as the literary essay *Ars Poetica*; and two books of Satires – the Latin word from which 'satire' comes had the meaning of a medley of reflections on social conditions and events, rather than of the pointed, witty vehicle of criticism with which it was later endowed.

From remarks in his own poems and from a biography by Suetonius, Horace appears to have been short and rotund, with dark hair that turned grey early. He seems to have been a bit of a hypochondriac, while enjoying to the full his life, his work, and the position his work gave him in society. He died only a few months after his patron Maecenas.

VIRGIL

The *Aeneid*, the epic of the empire of Rome and of Roman nationalism, for its poetry and poetic sensibility arguably the most influential poem in any language, is unfinished. Its author asked his friends, just before he died, to burn it. Literary executors, faced with just this problem throughout history, have usually responded with commendable common sense and regard to posterity, as they did in this case.

Publius Vergilius, or Virgilius, Maro (70–19 BC) was born near Mantua in Cisalpine Gaul, not far from the birthplace of Catullus. He had a good education in Cremona and Milan, and went on to study higher subjects, probably in Naples and Rome. He does not appear ever to have been very fit, and this may be one reason why he then returned to the family farm to write, only to be deprived of it in 41 BC in the confiscations after the battle of Philippi. He appealed against the decision and was reinstated on the orders of Octavian, but soon afterwards he left Mantua for good, first to live in a villa owned by his former tutor and then to live in Campania. In 37 BC he published his first major work, a series of bucolic episodes (the *Eclogues*) loosely based on a similar composition of the Hellenistic pastoral poet, Theocritus (*c.* 310–*c.* 250 BC). Maecenas gave him the encouragement to complete four books of didactic verse about farming and the country year called the *Georgics*, on which he spent the next seven years. Though these too show Greek influences, the agricultural activities (corn-growing, vine-culture, cattle-breeding, bee-keeping) are Italian and the message both topical and nationalistic, with its emphasis on traditional agricultural industries, on a return to the old forms of worship, and on co-operative working for a profitable future.

By this time Octavian was emperor in all but title and name. He felt that an epic poem about his own achievements – he was still only 33 – would be a suitable accompaniment to his eminence, and Maecenas (in his capacity as honorary minister of arts) approached several writers with the idea. They all turned it down, not necessarily because of any antipathy towards Augustus, to whom the Mediterranean world had much reason to be

156

grateful, but because epic was not their style. Virgil, however, accepted the assignment, but on his own terms. He knew what he wanted to do and saw this as the means to achieve it. He worked on his epic of the mythological antecedents of Rome

Figure 33 Though Virgil referred to the Britons as 'totally cut off from the whole world' (*Eclogues*, I. 66), Britain in Roman times was not entirely a cultural backwater. This fine fourth-century AD mosaic pavement, found at Low Ham in Somerset, illustrates incidents from the first and fourth books of the *Aeneid*. On the left, Aeneas's ships arrive on the African coast. At the top a naked Venus, goddess of love, presides over the meeting between Dido, queen of Carthage, and Aeneas, with Cupid, in the guise of Aeneas's son Ascanius, between them. On the right, Aeneas and the queen go hunting, and (bottom) sheltering together from the storm engineered by Juno, they embrace. In the central panel Venus stands between cupids with raised and lowered torches, signifying that Aeneas will live and Dido die. (*Somerset County Museums*)

until his death eleven years later, by which time he had composed some 10,000 lines. Augustus frequently asked after its progress and, apparently, was not disappointed with either the pace or the product. In the year 19 BC, Virgil met the emperor in Athens and, instead of going on a tour of Greece and the east as he had intended, accompanied him back to Rome. He caught a fever on the way and died a few days after landing at Brundisium. He was unmarried and, largely thanks to his patrons, a comparatively rich man; with commendable diplomacy he left considerable legacies to Maecenas and Augustus. Virgil always wrote in hexameters, and no one after him bettered his mastery of that medium.

The *Aeneid* is unfinished in that it awaited final revision and polishing. The story is complete and ends on a dramatic climax. Turnus, king of the Rutuli, stakes everything on single combat with Aeneas. They fight and Turnus is wounded. Aeneas is about to spare him, when he spots on his opponent's shoulder the belt of his dead ally and friend, Pallas, which Turnus has clearly stripped from the corpse in utter breach of mythological chivalry.

> . . . When the sight came home to him,
> Aeneas raged at the relic of his anguish
> Worn by the man as trophy. Blazing up
> And terrible in his anger, he called out:
> 'You in your plunder, torn from one of mine,
> Shall I be robbed of you? This wound will come
> From Pallas: Pallas makes this offering
> And from your criminal blood exacts his due.'
> He sank his blade in fury in Turnus' chest.
> Then all the body slackened in death's chill,
> And with a groan for that indignity
> His spirit fled into the gloom below.
> (*Aeneid*, XII. 945–52, tr. Robert Fitzgerald)

The story of the *Aeneid* is a deliberate continuation of Homer's *Iliad*, to stress the connection between Rome and the heroes of Troy, with strong echoes of the wanderings of Odysseus which are described in the *Odyssey*. The gods' continuous intervention and their periodic bickering as to which of their favourite mortals shall triumph are in tune with the traditional notions to which Augustus wanted his people to return.

To modern readers Aeneas may seem a character lacking in

personality: in 1914 the American poet and critic Ezra Pound described him as a 'stick'. To Virgil and his contemporaries Aeneas embodied the Stoic ideal, accepting all that fate threw at him and impassively pressing on towards his personal destiny. Literary debts to Virgil are legion. This pagan poet even became a prophet of Christianity: in the *Divine Comedy* of Dante (1265–1321), Virgil, in the personification of Human Reason, is the poet's guide to the Gates of Paradise. Among British poets who have implicitly or openly acknowledged his influence are Chaucer, Gavin Douglas, Marlowe, Shakespeare, Milton, Dryden (of course), Pope, Keats, and Tennyson. Nearer our own time, the American-born T. S. Eliot (1888–1965) wrote in his essay 'What is a Classic?' (1944):

> [Aeneas] is the symbol of Rome; and, as Aeneas is to Rome, so is ancient Rome to Europe. Thus Virgil acquires the centrality of the unique classic; he is at the centre of European civilization, in a position which no other poet can share or usurp.

ELEGIAC POETRY: PROPERTIUS AND OVID

Sextus Propertius (*c.* 50–*c.* 15 BC) was born near Assisi in Umbria, but his family, like Virgil's, was dispossessed in the proscriptions in 41 BC. His father died when he was a child, and his mother sent him to Rome to be educated for the law. Instead he turned to literature and published his first book of elegies in about 26 BC. Through this he acquired fame and an introduction to Maecenas, and though he resisted persuasion to compose patriotic verses, he was given the encouragement to write three more books before his early death from an unknown cause. Most of his poems describe his love for Cynthia, who in real life was called Hostia and appears to have been a freed-woman and a courtesan. Much of Propertius's poetry is peppered with academic allusions and pervaded with melancholy, but the emotions read as though they are sincerely expressed.

We have enough background for Publius Ovidius Naso (43 BC–AD 18), chiefly from evidence in his own poems, to form a picture of a literary philanderer; without knowing the reason why, at the height of his powers and his popularity, he was banished by Augustus, as it turned out for life, to the Roman equivalent of

Siberia, a small bleak place called Tomi (modern Constanţa) on the west coast of the Black Sea.

Ovid was born at Sulmo, in the mountains east of Rome, of an ancient equestrian family. Destined for a political career, he studied rhetoric and law, and was married at about 16 and divorced shortly afterwards. After doing a grand tour of Greece, Asia Minor, and Sicily, accompanied by a companion/ tutor, he held minor legal and administrative posts in the civil service, but abandoned politics for poetry in about 16 BC, when he married again – his wife died two years later, having had a daughter. He combined his pursuits of poetry and pleasure in *Amores* (Love Poems) and *Ars Amatoria* (The Art of Love). These were not so much erotic as irresponsible in that they appeared to condone adultery, which under Augustan law was a public offence and on which Augustus himself was rather touchy, especially as he had in 2 BC to banish his own daughter, Julia, for just that.

Ars Amatoria was published in 1 BC; nine years later, Augustus's granddaughter Julia followed her mother into exile for the same reason. Ovid says (*Tristia*, II. 207) that the reasons for his summary removal from the scene were 'a poem' (presumably *Ars Amatoria*) and 'an error'. Since that book had appeared so many years earlier, we must look to the error for the clue to the mystery. It may have had something to do with the younger Julia – there is no reason why an impressionable and sexually voracious young woman should not have been attracted to a poet in his fifties – or possibly someone disclosed some scandal about Ovid and her mother. Whatever it was, Ovid had to go, and *Ars Amatoria* was banned from Rome's three public libraries. He was never called back, even after the death of Augustus, though he kept writing, sadly and ultimately resignedly.

A region that neighbours the polar constellations
  imprisons me now, land seared by crimping frost.
To the north lie Bosporus, Don, the Scythian marshes, a scatter
  of names in an all-but-unknown waste:
beyond that, nothing but frozen, uninhabitable tundra –
  alas, how close I stand to the world's end!
Remote, though, from my homeland, remote from my beloved
  wife, and all else I once enjoyed: I can't
make physical contact with them, must imagine their presence,

see them all in my mind's eye,
visions of home, the City, familiar landscapes
    each with its cluster of memories. My wife's
image – visible, real, as though she were present –
    both aggravates and lightens my distress:
aggravates it through her absence, lightens it by bearing
    her burden with constancy, by her gift of love.

(Tristia, III. 4, 46–62, tr. Peter Green)

His third wife, a young widow with a daughter, whom he
married in about AD 2, remained devoted to him to the last.

Figure 34 Part of a wall painting from Pompeii of the legend of Europa
and the bull, one of the many stories of transformation woven into Ovid's
Metamorphoses (II. 837–75). Europa, daughter of the king of Phoenicia,
was attracted by a fine white bull while she played with her companions.
It was Zeus in disguise, acting so tame that she was tempted to climb on
to his back. He carried her away over the sea to Crete, where he revealed
himself to her. They had three sons, who were adopted by the king of
Crete, to whom Zeus then married her off. (*C. M. Dixon*)

Ovid aimed to use elegiac couplets to amuse the reader, which he did as much by verbal effects and ingenious and delicate deployment of his verse form as by what he said. The fifteen books of *Metamorphoses* (Transformations), his most lasting and influential work, are written in hexameters. This vast collection of linked myths and legends was widely drawn upon by later Roman and European writers, including Chaucer and John Gower (*c*. 1330–1408), and parts of it were translated into English by William Caxton (1480) and Dryden (1699). Like many good writers, Ovid appears to have had a blind spot about the quality of some of his work. Seneca the Elder (*c*. 55 BC–*c*. AD 37), father of the philosopher, tells how friends of Ovid once asked the poet if he would allow them to suggest which three lines might most readily be omitted from his published work. He agreed, if he might nominate the three most deserving of immortality. It transpired that the lines were in each case the same!

EPIGRAM AND SATIRE: MARTIAL AND JUVENAL

An epigram is a Greek term meaning 'inscription', often in verse, on a tombstone or accompanying an offering. Subsequently it came to stand for almost any occasional short poem. The form was widely used in Rome, until, in the hands of Martial, it became the medium for short, pointed, witty sayings about people and the hazards of daily and social life, usually in elegiacs, but also in hendecasyllabics and other metres. Marcus Valerius Martialis (*c*. AD 40–104) was a Spaniard from Bilbilis who came to Rome in AD 64 and was taken up by his literary fellow-countrymen, Seneca and his nephew Lucan, until in the following year they were purged by Nero. Martial lived in a third-floor flat on the slope of the Quirinal Hill, scraping a living by writing verses for anybody and any occasion, even on labels for gifts which guests took away from a party. The verses ultimately did well, for he published several books of them, and ended up owning a farm in the country as well as a house in Rome. He was a hack, a parasite, and, when it suited his interests, as it did when writing about Domitian, an unctuous flatterer. That did not prevent him, however, from being almost always witty, if often coarse, and frequently poetic, while

162

pioneering a form of literature which has had, and still has, many exponents.

One of Martial's friends – if a man of his nature and bent can be said to have any – was Decimus Junius Juvenalis (*c.* AD 55–*c.* 140), most graphic of the Roman satirists and the last of the classical poets of Rome. As far as we can tell, he was born in Aquinum, the son of a well-to-do Spanish freedman; he may have served as commander of an auxiliary cohort in Britain and have held civic offices in his home town before trying to make a living in Rome by public speaking. At some point during the reign of Domitian, he seems to have been exiled for a while to Egypt, undoubtedly for saying or writing something offensive to the emperor, but not offensive enough to be executed for it. The sixteen Satires that we have, however, were published between about AD 110 and 130, in the reigns of Trajan and Hadrian. Written in hexameters, they attack various social targets, including homosexuals, living conditions in Rome, women, extravagance, human parasites, and vanity, while moralizing on such subjects as learning, guilty consciences, parental example, and the treatment of civilians by the military. There is sarcasm, invective, and broad humour, though of a kind which in modern terms would be the stocks-in-trade of a crusading journalist rather than of a satirical poet. Yet, as one reads the fourth satire, a ridiculous account of Domitian summoning a council of state to deliberate upon what should be done with a prize turbot, with which he has been presented as his due, it seems more pointed in the light of a newspaper report in 1986 of a sturgeon caught in British territorial waters. It was sold to a restaurateur, who remembered, just in time, an ancient law whereby all sturgeons belonged to the Crown. As a formality, he offered the fish to Her Majesty the Queen. The Palace replied that she would accept it.

THE NOVEL: PETRONIUS AND APULEIUS

The romance in prose was a literary form used by the Greeks in the second century AD. In the hands of two Roman writers in particular, the novel took on a very different aspect. Hovering between prose fiction and satire in its senses both of 'medley' and 'ridicule' is the *Satyricon* of Gaius Petronius (d. AD 66), known also as Petronius Arbiter from his rather inappropriate job title of

Elegantiae Arbiter (Judge of Taste), in which capacity he organized Nero's personal revels. *Satyricon* is also the original picaresque novel, a kind of bisexual odyssey of two men and their boy round the towns of southern Italy. We only have fragments, the best-known being 'Trimalchio's Dinner-Party', which though delib-erately overdrawn nevertheless splendidly exhibits the manners and *mores* of the Roman *nouveaux riches*.

> Trimalchio . . . at the top of his voice declared that now was the time for anyone who wanted a second glass of mead. Then a sudden crash from the band gave the cue and all the dishes of the first course were whisked away by a troop of singing slaves. One of the side-dishes was dropped in the flurry and a slave-boy picked it up from the floor. Trimalchio noticed him, gave orders for a clout on the ear to punish him, and made him throw the dish back where it had fallen. A litter-slave came promptly in and set to work sweeping the silver out with a broom among the other rubbish and scraps. Then two fuzzy-haired Ethiopians entered with small wine-skins, like those used for scattering sand in an amphitheatre, and squirted out wine for washing our hands. No one offered us water.
>
> (*Cena Trimalchionis*, XXXIV, tr. Jack Lindsay)

Petronius, victim of one of Nero's periodic purges, died with considerable style and urbanity. According to Tacitus, he bled himself slowly to death, while conversing, eating, and even sleeping, having committed to paper 'a list of Nero's most perverted acts, classified according to the novelty of the perfor-mance, with male as well as female partners, and their names, which he dispatched to the emperor under seal' (*Annals*, XVI. 19).

Lucius Apuleius was born in about AD 125 at Madaura in North Africa. According to his own account, he married a rich widow much older than himself, and was then accused by her family of sorcery – he was certainly much interested in magic and its effects. He conducted his own defence and was acquitted. His novel *Metamorphoses*, better known as *The Golden Ass*, is a rollicking tale of the supernatural, told in the first person, of how Lucius tries to dabble in magic, is given the wrong ointment by the serving-maid who is also his bed-mate, and is turned into an ass. Several good stories are spliced into the action, including an excellent version of the legend of Cupid and Psyche. The conversion of Lucius to the cult of Isis after his re-transformation into human form gives the ending a religious significance as well as a narrative twist. Apuleius himself became a priest of Osiris and Isis, and was also a devotee of Asclepius, god of medicine, which he seems to have found compatible with organizing gladiatorial shows for the province of Africa.

HISTORIANS: CAESAR, LIVY, TACITUS, SUETONIUS

The original Roman records, with the names of the principal officials for each year, were inscribed on white tablets in the keeping of the *pontifex maximus* and displayed to public view. The first historian who wrote in Latin was Cato the Elder, but his history of Rome is lost. The earliest surviving account of contemporary events is the seven books of Julius Caesar's own record of his campaigns in Gaul, *De Bello Gallico* (Gallic War) – an eighth book was written by Aulus Hirtius (*d.* 43 BC), one of Caesar's officers. Objective in that he mentions but does not dwell on his failures, and written in the third person, it is a distinguished general's account of his actions in war in a clear, no-nonsense style, to be read and studied, rather than listened to. The arts of the orator and politician are more evident in *De Bello Civili* (Civil War), in which by careful selection of facts and by linguistic legerdemain he attempts to put the blame squarely on the shoulders of his opponents.

Titus Livius (59 BC–AD 17) was born and died in Padua, lived most of his life in Rome, had two children, and was a close acquaintance of Augustus and Claudius, the latter of whom he encouraged to write history. That is just about all we know about this great writer and moderately good historian, whose reputation in his time was such that it is said that a Spaniard came all the way from Cadiz to Rome just to look at him, and, having done so, went back home satisfied. Livy's full history of Rome from Aeneas to 9 BC comprised 142 books, of which we have thirty-five, plus synopses of the others. He was a popular historian in that he concentrated on narrative and character, and paid particular attention to the composition of the speeches he put into the mouths of his protagonists. He drew on a wide range of sources and traditions without being particularly concerned about their accuracy, though he makes up for vagueness about geographical and military details with his sense of drama. The truth he sought was that offering moral lessons from the past which would in turn reflect gloriously on the Rome of the present.

> The task of writing a history of our nation from Rome's earliest days fills me, I confess, with some misgiving. . . . I am aware that for historians to make extravagant claims is, and always has been, all too common: every writer on history tends to look down his nose at his less cultivated predecessors, happily persuaded that he will better them in point of style, or bring new facts to light. But however that may be, I shall find satisfaction in contributing – not, I hope, too ignobly – to the labour of putting on record the story of the greatest nation in the world . . . .
>
> My task, moreover, is an immensely laborious one. I shall have to go back more than seven hundred years, and trace my story from its small beginnings up to these recent times when its ramifications are so vast that any adequate treatment is hardly possible. I am aware, too, that most readers will take less pleasure in my account of how Rome began and in her early history; they will wish to hurry on to more modern times and read of the period, already a long one, in which the might of an imperial people is beginning to work its own ruin. My own feeling is different; I shall find antiquity a rewarding study, if only because, while I am absorbed in it, I shall be able to turn my eyes from the troubles which for so long have tormented the modern world, and to write without any of that over-anxious consideration which may well plague a writer on contemporary life, even if it does not lead him to conceal the truth.
>
> (*History of Rome*, I. Preface, tr. Aubrey de Sélincourt)

Cornelius Tacitus (*c.* AD 55–*c.* 117) was a public figure in his own right as well as being the son-in-law of Agricola. He was a senator, consul in AD 97, and governor of Asia in AD 112. He was an excellent public speaker, and published a book on oratory when he was in his twenties. Of two series of histories covering the reign of Tiberius to that of Domitian, we have just a few books, known respectively as the 'Histories' and the 'Annals'. He also wrote a short, somewhat flattering biography of Agricola, and *Germania*, a graphic report on the land and people of Germany. He was a witty writer as well as an incisive literary stylist, a shrewd observer and commentator, and an upholder of the ancient virtues of his nation.

> The preceding period of 820 years dating from the foundation of Rome has found many historians. So long as republican history was their theme, they wrote with equal eloquence of style and independence of outlook. But when the Battle of Actium had been fought and the interests of peace demanded the concentration of power in the hands of one man, this great line of classical historians came to an end. Truth, too, suffered in more ways than one. To an understandable ignorance of policy, which now lay outside public control, was in due course added a passion for flattery, or else a hatred of autocrats. Thus neither school bothered about posterity, for the one was bitterly alienated and the other deeply committed. But whereas the reader can easily discount the bias of the time-serving historian, detraction and spite find a ready audience. Adulation bears the ugly taint of subservience, but malice gives the false impression of being independent. My official career owed its beginnings to Vespasian, its progress to Titus, and its further advancement to Domitian. I have no wish to deny this. But partiality and hatred towards any man are equally inappropriate in a writer who claims to be honest and reliable.
>
> (*Histories*, I. 1, tr. Kenneth Wellesley)

Just over four books of the *Histories* survive, describing the years AD 69–70: the brief reigns of Galba, Otho, and Vitellius, and the beginning of that of Vespasian. Of the *Annals*, we have books covering parts of the reigns of Tiberius, Claudius, and Nero. Ammianus Marcellinus (*c.* AD 330–*c.* 393) wrote a continuation of the histories of Tacitus in thirty-one books, of which we have eighteen, covering just the years AD 353–78. Tacitus's writings were lost until the fifteenth century: thereafter his political thought influenced the Italian statesman Niccolo Machiavelli (1469–1527), and his literary style the French essayist Michel de Montaigne (1533–92), while his philosophic attitude to history is reflected in the monumental and memorable *History of the Decline and Fall of the Roman Empire* by Edward Gibbon (1737–94).

The family of Gaius Suetonius Tranquillus (*c*. AD 70–*c*. 140) probably came from Algiers. They were of equestrian class, and his father had a distinguished military career. He himself held a succession of posts in the imperial court, becoming director of the imperial libraries and then chief of Hadrian's personal secretariat, which gave him access to archive material on earlier reigns. His series of biographies of the Caesars is the only one of his many biographical and antiquarian works to have survived intact. He was, with Plutarch, for better or for worse the originator of the modern biography.

PHILOSOPHY AND SCIENCE: SENECA AND PLINY THE ELDER

We have already met Lucius Annaeus Seneca (4 BC–AD 65) as the tutor, and victim, of the emperor Nero and as the first patron of Martial. The second son of Seneca 'the Elder' or 'the Rhetorician', he was born in Corduba in Spain, of a brilliant family. He was brought to Rome at an early age and was influenced by the Stoics, whose philosophy ran counter to that of the Epicureans in that its keynote was 'duty' rather than 'pleasure', and it allowed for the existence of an overall spiritual intelligence. Seneca's pretensions to being a practising philosopher are questionable: he condoned various dynastic murders, was banished for eight years under suspicion of having an affair with one of Caligula's sisters (during which time both his first wife and his son died), and, on his return, while undoubtedly but temporarily curbing the worst excesses of his pupil Nero, grew rich in the process.

In his philosophical writings, however, of which twelve dialogues and 124 'Epistles' to his friend Lucilius survive, he comes across as a moral philosopher whose aim was to live correctly through the exercise of reason. *Naturales Quaestiones* (Scientific Investigations) is an examination of natural phenomena from the point of view of a Stoic philosopher. *Apocolocyntosis*, by contrast, is a wicked skit on the dead Claudius. We also have ten of his verse tragedies: solid, lyrical, and bleak in their tragic vision which allows no escape from evil or defence against the brutality of fate. From his example, Elizabethan and Jacobean dramatists took the five-act structure and also the cast of secondary characters who serve to keep the action moving, to report on events off-stage, and to elicit private thoughts (especially those of the heroine through a female confidante). The violent and gruesome *Thyestes* is the archetypal revenge tragedy, such as Kyd, Tourneur, and to a certain extent Shakespeare in *Hamlet*, exploited.

It was natural phenomena with which Gaius Plinius Secundus (AD 23–79), Pliny the Elder, was concerned throughout his life and at the time of his accidental death. He was born at Como of a wealthy family, practised law in Rome, and saw military service through several postings (during which he began a twenty-book history of the German wars). He probably went to ground during the reign of Nero, returning to public life on the accession of Vespasian in AD 70. Between then and his death nine years later he not only held several senior government posts, including that of deputy governor of northern Spain, but wrote a further thirty books of Roman history and the thirty-seven books of his 'Natural History'. This, his only surviving work, covers many subjects, including physics, geography, ethnology, physiology, zoology, botany, medicine, and metallurgy, with frequent digressions into anything else which interested him at the time. He drew his material from many written sources – when he was not actually reading something himself or writing, he had someone read aloud to him – as well as from his own observations. For example, in Book XX, on 'medicines derived from garden plants', he lists 1,606 drugs and cites the works of fifty-two writers as sources. He always carried a notebook, as he did on the expedition from the naval station at Misenum, of which he was then in command, to investigate from closer at hand the eruption of Vesuvius. He went ashore on the beach, taking notes all the time, and was either asphyxiated by the fumes or buried under falling rocks.

LETTER WRITERS: CICERO AND PLINY THE YOUNGER

Of Cicero the man, the political and forensic orator, and the statesman, something has already been said, and a number of speeches, and also philosophical works, in which field he established a tradition of Roman writing, survive from the hand of this master of style and rhetoric. To the student of Roman life, however, the four collections of his letters, edited shortly after his death in 43 BC, are of even greater and more immediate interest: 'To his Brother Quintus', a soldier and provincial governor who also died in the proscriptions; 'To his Friends'; 'To Brutus', the conspirator; and 'To Atticus', who was Cicero's closest friend and confidant. Some of these letters were undoubtedly intended for ultimate publication – what public and literary figure does not have this eventuality in mind? – but, taken as a whole, they are refreshingly revealing about himself and his day-to-day existence during the last twenty-five years of his life.

Gaius Plinius Caecilius Secundus (AD 61–c. 113), known as Pliny the Younger to distinguish him from his even more eminent and industrious uncle and adoptive father, certainly did intend his correspondence for publication, and in his lifetime, too. He showed early literary promise – he wrote a tragedy in Greek verse when he was 13 – and became a distinguished orator, public servant, and philanthropist. He was three times married, and though he had no children he was awarded, as Martial and Suetonius had been, honorary status as a 'three-child parent', a privilege originally bestowed by Augustus on genuine qualifiers, which brought certain privileges including exemption from taxes. Not that Pliny had any need of money. He was exceedingly rich: he endowed a library at Como, a school for children of free-born parents, and a public baths, while the interest on an even larger sum was left in his will for the benefit of 100 freedmen and for an annual public banquet. His letters range over many private and public topics; of especial interest is his first-hand account of the eruption of Vesuvius (VI. 16 and 20), the description of his villa (II. 17), news of a haunted house in Athens (VII. 27) and of a tame dolphin (IX. 33), and his official report to Trajan (X. 97), in his capacity as governor of Bithynia in Asia Minor, on the Christians and his request for a policy decision on how to deal with them.

8

THE ROMAN ARMY

The Roman talent for organization is nowhere better illustrated than by its army, the backbone of which was that epitome of the professional fighting man, the legionary. After the civil war, Augustus created a standing army of twenty-eight legions, at which strength, give or take the odd legion, it remained for 200 years. He also increased the length of service from six to sixteen years, with a further four years on lighter duties.

THE LEGION

Under the republic, new legions were assigned a serial number, numbers I to IV being reserved for those raised by consuls: those levied elsewhere were allocated higher numbers. Whatever the system, and it is still not fully understood, at any one time several legions might have the same number. To avoid confusion, each came to assume also a title or nickname, reflecting the circumstances of its formation, the name of its founder, the place where it was raised, or the front where it had served with distinction. There was a First German as well as a First Italian legion: similarly a Second Parthian and a Second Trajan's Brave. The Tenth United was formed from two original legions. The Ninth Hispana (i.e. Spanish), once thought to have disappeared in Britain, possibly in Scotland, appears now to have been transferred to Germany in about AD 115. A legion's own standard, often referred to as its 'eagle', was carried wherever it went. The eagle was the rallying point for troops in battle and a signal as to where the action was: to lose it to the enemy was both a disaster and a disgrace. The *aquilifer*, who carried the legion's standard, ranked in seniority only just below a centurion and

171

was responsible also for the safe-keeping of the legion's pay-chest. The *imaginifer* bore a second standard, made up of medallions of reigning and deified emperors. Both wore animal skins over their uniforms, with the heads drawn up over their helmets.

A legion was a self-contained unit which even on the march could rely on its own resources for weeks on end. The legionaries themselves did all the manual work of digging, construction, and engineering. Every man carried trenching tools and a pair of stakes which at each stop became part of the camp palisade. He also had to shoulder, or carry attached to his person, clothes, a cooking-pot, rations, and any personal possessions, as well as his weapons and armour. Marius is credited with the invention of a fork-shaped contrivance to ease the burden: the aspect of the legionaries as they marched along earned them the sobriquet 'Marius's Mules'.

Each legion had a complement of specialists and craftsmen, known collectively as *immunes*, 'excused from normal duties': surveyors, medical and veterinary orderlies, armourers, carpenters, hunters, even soothsayers. The surveyors went ahead of the column of march to select and lay out the site of the night's camp; it was always constructed to the same pattern and surrounded by a ditch, a rampart, and a palisade, all of which had to be built afresh each time. Leather tents, each of which slept eight men, were carried separately by mules. At legionary headquarters or in the forts that defended the empire there was a wider range of non-combatant staff, including clerks to look after and process the paperwork, paymasters, and military police.

In the field, a legion consisted of ten cohorts, each divided up into six centuries of eighty men, under the command of a centurion. The commander of a legion (*legatus*) held his post usually for three to four years, as a prelude to a provincial governorship; he was assisted by six younger officers, the military tribunes. These, too, were short-term political appointees; the next step up for the senior tribune (*tribunus laticlavius*) was a seat in the senate. The senior professional soldier in the legion was likely to be the camp prefect (*praefectus castrorum*). He was usually a man of some thirty years' service, and was responsible for organization, training, and equipment. Day-to-day responsibility was therefore in the hands of the centurions, the most senior of whom (*centurio primus pilus*) commanded the first century of the first cohort. Centurions did not march; they rode on horseback, and they had powers of corporal punishment – the twisted vine-staff each carried was not just an emblem of rank.

OTHER UNITS

The legions were supported by auxiliary forces, composed of inhabitants of the empire who were not citizens of Rome, and who often brought their own military skills to add bite to time-honoured Roman infantry tactics. All squadrons of cavalry were auxiliaries, each one divided up into troops of thirty men. While some auxiliaries fought as infantry and were equipped like legionaries, others retained their native dress and weapons, and served as archers, slingers, spearmen, or broadswordsmen. Originally auxiliaries were led by their own chiefs, but in imperial times they were brought within an overall chain of command under Roman officers. From the reign of Claudius, an auxiliary and his immediate family qualified for Roman citizenship after twenty-five years' service, which constituted a further extension of social mobility.

Under the empire, the only armed forces in Italy were the *cohors praetoria* (the imperial guard), and the *cohortes urbanae* (city cohorts), who garrisoned Rome itself and whose presence was to prevent unrest rather than ward off possible attack from outside, which was unthinkable. The imperial guard was a crack unit whose members wore a special uniform and received double pay, in addition to the bribes which they came to be offered in the guise of bonuses for their allegiance. When the emperor went on campaign, the imperial guard went with him. A further force, the *vigiles*, recruited from freedmen, patrolled Rome itself and served as its fire brigade.

Up to the time of Augustus, mastery of the seas had been achieved by *ad hoc* measures and largely foreign naval skills and crews – no Roman citizen ever handled an oar. Augustus established a standing fleet of about 700 ships which were his own property and which he manned with slaves and freedmen of his personal service. His successors saw the wisdom of his initiative, and under the emperor's overall command there were established a number of regional flotillas: two for Italy (based at Misenum and Ravenna), and the rest to help exercise control over the provinces, centred on Egypt, Syria, Cyrenaica, the

Figure 35   A relief in the Louvre from the period of Trajan and Hadrian, showing members of the imperial guard, indicated by their rich uniforms and helmets, and oval shields. Behind is a legionary standard, with the eagle holding a thunderbolt in its claws. (*Deutsches Archaeologisches Institut, Rome*)

Black Sea, the Danube, the Rhine, and Boulogne. This last, the British flotilla, was used by Agricola in AD 83 to soften up the opposition in Scotland by making lightning raids up the east coast; it also (according to Tacitus) discovered the Orkney islands and established conclusively that Britain was an island.

WEAPONS AND TACTICS

The deployment of the Roman infantry in battle depended on its mobility. Apart from his hob-nailed heavy sandals, a legionary's legs were bare except in the colder climates, where tight-fitting knee-breeches were the order of the day. The most usual form of helmet was bronze, with a skull-cap inside and projections to protect the back of the neck and the ears and cheeks. A legionary carried on his left arm the cylindrical leather shield, which was shaped to fit his body and was about 1.2 metres long. It was also useful as a siege weapon; a body of men crouched underneath their locked-together shields could approach a wall undeterred by missiles from above. Not unnaturally, this formation was known as the 'tortoise'. On the march a man carried two javelins of different weights, each 2 metres long and with a metal head. One of these went into battle with him; he hurled it at the enemy when in range, before getting down to the serious business of fighting hand to hand with his short, double-edged, thrusting and stabbing sword.

Battles were largely fought with 'conventional' weapons. The artillery of the time, of which the largest and most effective weapon was known as the *onager* (wild ass) because of its kick, was used as siege batteries. Each century, however, was allocated a mechanical arrow-shooter which was deployed in battle. A Roman general's objective was to break up and, if possible, break through the enemy lines by sheer force of concerted numbers and by manipulating his infantry. Horsemen were mainly employed to head off attacks by the opposition's cavalry and to pursue stragglers. Julius Caesar's favoured tactic was to draw up his cohorts in three lines, each some eight men deep. His first victory in Gaul, at Bibracte in 58 BC, was achieved without the use of cavalry and by a manoeuvre which could only have succeeded when performed by highly trained and disciplined troops.

CONSOLIDATING AND PATROLLING THE EMPIRE

In republican times, the empire had been allowed to expand as opportunity, circumstances, and the senate decreed. Augustus recognized the need for a specific foreign policy and saw that

The Battle of Bibracte 58BC

Figure 36 The battle of Bibracte 58 BC

Caesar drew up his four legions in three lines (R). The Helvetii, in close-
packed columns, advanced and attacked (H), but were thrown into
confusion by the Roman javelins. Then Caesar advanced. The Helvetii
retired to a hill to the north (H2). Caesar wheeled to face them, but was
attacked in the rear by a force of Boii and Tulingi, who had then arrived
on the scene (B, T). The first two Roman lines remained facing the
Helvetii (R2), who returned to the attack (H3). The third Roman line
faced about (R3). Both enemy forces were defeated and the Helvetii fled.

to undertake random wars of aggression, and often of attrition,
in pursuit of new conquests was an uneconomic and unsatisfac-
tory way of exercising it. Military success, however, was a Roman
way of life, but he would ensure that it was gained by consolidat-
ing provinces and their defences, without enabling any commander to aspire to an overwhelming personal following among his

troops. The frontiers of the empire developed according to the lines to which he had withdrawn following the Varian disaster in AD 9, when Publius Quintilius Varus lost three complete legions, three cavalry regiments, and six auxiliary cohorts, after being enticed into unfamiliar territory between the rivers Weser and Ems by a chieftain of the Cherusci, Arminius (81 BC–AD 19), a Roman equestrian who had now rebelled against Rome. Varus committed suicide, the Romans retired permanently to the west bank of the Rhine, and new Germanic tribes moved into the region which they had vacated.

Tiberius was advised by Augustus not to try to extend the boundaries of the empire. His immediate successors were either too suspicious or too frightened of the army to do much else, with one notable exception, Claudius's invasion of Britain in AD 43. Three years earlier Claudius had altered the status of Mauretania from client kingdom to two provinces. Thrace, too, had been a client kingdom in the time of Augustus, and in AD 46 Claudius defused an ugly situation by making it a province. That was that, as far as the extent of the empire was concerned, for more than fifty years, until in AD 101 Trajan crossed the river Danube into Dacia, without waiting to give a chance to the treaty agreed between Domitian and Decebalus, king of Dacia. This resulted in a great victory but dubious long-term advantage (though modern Romanian is one of the Romance languages, derived from Latin), and Dacia was finally evacuated of Roman troops in AD 275. In AD 106 Trajan assumed into Roman 'protection' the area which became the province of Arabia and which controlled the main caravan route to the coast of Palestine. In AD 114 and 115 he also annexed Armenia as far as the Persian Gulf, and made further inroads into Mesopotamia, but these were tactical acts of immediate military expediency which were promptly reversed by his successor, Hadrian, in AD 117.

Some legions remained on the same station for many years; others were deployed as the situation demanded. The Second Augusta, raised by Augustus himself, and the Twentieth Valeria Victrix (Strong and Victorious) spearheaded the invasion of Britain in AD 43; they were among the last to be evacuated in AD 400, though a detachment from the Twentieth was sent to Mainz on the Rhine in AD 270 to help deal with troubles there. The Twentieth was also Agricola's strike-force in northern

Mons Graupius
Inchtuthil
Antonine Wall
Hadrian's Wall
BRITAIN
York
Chester
St Albans
Bath ● London ● Colchester
R. Weser *Cherusci*
R. Ems
R. Elbe
R. Rhine
Rheims ● *Marcomanni* Mainz
Paris ● Trier ● *Franks*
GERMANY *Quadi*
Alesia *Alamanni*
GAUL
RAETIA
Bibracte ●
Lugdunum
R. Rhône Aquileia
Avignon
SPAIN *R. Ebro* Orange
Clunia ● Numantia Nimes ● Arles Ariminum
Bilbilis ● Salona
Massilia
Alcantara ● CORSICA
Rome ●
Saguntum ●
Italica ● Corduba ● SARDINIA
Munda ●

MEDITERRANEAN SEA

Drepanum
MAURETANIA Carthage ● SICILY
Zama ● Syracuse
Numidia

AFRICA

Leptis Magna ●

THE ROMAN EMPIRE *c.* AD 130
DURING THE REIGN OF HADRIAN
(including places outside Italy mentioned in the book)

R. Vistula

Alani

Vandals

R. Dnieper

Huns

R. Dniester

NORICUM
} *Goths*
PANNONIA   DACIA
R. Danube

ILLYRICUM   Tomi
(DALMATIA)   MOESIA   *BLACK SEA*
Sea of   Bosporus
Naissus   Marmara
THRACE   Byzantium   PONTUS   ARMENIA
MACEDONIA   Philippi   Nicomedia   Zela
Brundisium Apollonia   BITHYNIA
EPIRUS   Nicaea
Pharsalus Thessalonica Troy (Pergamum) GALATIA
Actium   Chalcis   ASIA   MESOPOTAMIA
Argos   Ephesus   CAPPADOCIA
ACHAEA   Issus
LYCIA   CILICIA   R. Euphrates
Delos   Phoenicia
Eleusis   Rhodes   SYRIA   Palmyra
CYPRUS

CRETE
PALESTINE (JUDAEA)

Nazareth
Alexandria   Jerusalem
Masada
CYRENAICA   ARABIA
EGYPT

Britain, and his successor constructed the fortress at Inchtuthil in Perthshire as its headquarters. This, the most northern of all Roman permanent fortifications, occupied an area 457 metres square and was to have been a purpose-built city in miniature, with streets and full administrative, residential, and leisure amenities, including separate houses for each of the officers and a hospital containing sixty five-bedded wards opening off each side of a wide corridor of the rectangular building. While still under construction, it was abandoned and systematically destroyed to prevent anything falling into the hands of the enemy.

Originally, the extent of the occupation of a region was bounded by a *limes* (plural *limites*), which just meant a 'path' or 'track'. Then it came to refer to the military road which linked the permanent forts housing units of a legion, whose task it was to discourage hostile military gatherings beyond the 'line', keep the peace and encourage Romanization within it, and allow free movement for trade across it. Thus *limes* came to mean 'boundary' or 'frontier' and the English word derived from it to signify something which 'may not be passed'. Sometimes, as in the case of Hadrian's Wall and the Antonine Wall in Britain, the *limes* was an actual wall. Hadrian was responsible, too, for reviewing the physical boundaries of the whole empire. He strengthened with a wooden palisade the defences of the Rhine which, together with those on the upper Danube, already consisted of 170 forts and fortresses. In Africa, where problems could be expected from cavalry, he devised a combination of a deep wide ditch and a low stone wall.

9

END OF AN EMPIRE

The extinction of the Julio-Claudian and Flavian dynasties did not bring an end to a consistent policy of rule or to dynastic succession. It simply meant that the two were never again effectively combined. Able men were, however, able to make their way to the very top from modest beginnings, and, if allowed to reign without internecine upheaval, could do so with as much insight and flair as any of the Caesars, and with more than most.

THE 'FIVE GOOD EMPERORS' AD 96-180

When for the first time the senate made its own choice of emperor and appointed Nerva, its members not only chose well, but ensured that equal perspicacity would attend the selection of his four successors. There was to be a further break with tradition, for all four came from families which had long before settled out of Italy: those of Trajan, Hadrian, and Marcus Aurelius in Spain, and that of Antoninus in Gaul. Nerva was 64 when he was pitchforked into supreme power, but, like a number of stop-gap rulers in more recent times, he performed wisely and courageously. He vowed publicly that he would never execute a member of the senate, and stuck to his promise, even when the senator Calpurnius Crassus was proved guilty of conspiracy against him. He not only assured himself of the support of the military by adopting as his son and joint ruler the distinguished commander in Upper Germany, Marcus Ulpius Trajanus (Trajan), but set an important precedent by nominating Trajan as his successor.

Trajan, who was born at Italica near Seville in AD 52, became

181

Figure 37 Gold *aureus* of the time of Trajan, with the head of his wife, Plotina. Imperial consorts, and sometimes imperial daughters and nieces, as well as mothers, appear on coins of their times. It was said in some quarters that Plotina engineered Trajan's final adoption of Hadrian as his son and kept her husband's death a secret until an official bulletin about the adoption had been issued. (×2)

emperor in AD 98, and was thus of an age of considerable discretion. He demonstrated this at once by establishing that the senate would always be kept informed about what was going on, and that the sovereign right to rule was compatible with freedom for those who were ruled. That he was a brilliant general is clear from his military exploits, but he was also a good person to work for, of which there is evidence in the correspondence between him and Pliny the Younger, especially when the latter was governor of Bithynia. Pliny frequently asks for advice on matters which are outside his immediate experience. The replies are invariably sound and diplomatic.

Trajan perhaps exercised less discretion in his choice of military campaigns, though they brought him considerable glory. After the triumphal procession with which he celebrated his first victory over the Dacians in AD 103, there were 123 days of public games and gladiatorial contests. He also determined to subdue the troublesome Parthians, who occupied great tracts of rugged desert land south of the Caspian Sea. He scored some notable victories and occupied some of the Parthian lands, but fell ill and died on his way back to Rome in AD 117, having left his chief-of-staff, Publius Aelius Hadrianus (Hadrian), who was born in AD 76 and who was his ward, in charge of the inconclusive situation in the east.

Hadrian claimed that Trajan had adopted him on his deathbed: in any case he had already been acclaimed as emperor by the army in the east, and the senate had little choice but to confirm him in the post or risk civil war. In the face of widespread revolts in regions which Trajan had conquered, Hadrian abandoned the recent acquisitions in the east and settled down to restore general order throughout the empire and to consolidate the administration at home. The wall in Britain which bears his name, and of which portions still survive, is a monument to and a reminder of the role he took upon himself as ruler of an empire. It was, in fact, less of an empire as we understand the term than a collection of territories occupied by Roman troops and administered by Roman citizens according to Roman law. Because of distances, difficulties of communication, and widely differing circumstances, central government from Rome was well-nigh impossible, and provincial governors were largely left to their own devices. Hadrian, however, travelled tirelessly not only to all the provinces of Rome, but along most of their outer confines as well, and established boundary lines. He was a man of wide learning, who, it was said, spoke Greek more fluently than Latin, was a patron of art, literature, and education, and a benefactor of the needy poor. His liberal-mindedness did not, however, extend to the Jews, whom he provoked into renewed revolt by forbidding Jewish practices, including circumcision, and by building a shrine to Jupiter on the site in Jerusalem where the ancient Jewish temple had stood before it was gutted and demolished by Titus. The rising, under Simon Bar Kochba (d. AD 135) in AD 131, was surprisingly effective, and was only put down after Hadrian had transferred Sextus Julius Severus, governor of Britain, to the Judaean front as commander. If the account of Dio Cassius is accurate, in order to stop the threat of further war, the Roman army destroyed fifty Jewish fortresses and 985 villages, and killed 580,000 men. The 82-year-old Rabbi Akiba, and other scholars and teachers who had supported Bar Kochba, were tortured and then executed.

Hadrian died in AD 138. Once again, the childlessness of the emperor worked to the benefit of the state. After his first choice as successor died, Hadrian had just before his own death adopted in his place the eminent senator Antoninus, then in his early fifties. At the same time he restricted the choice of the next emperor after Antoninus to Lucius Verus (AD 130–69), son of his original nominee, or Antoninus's own nephew Marcus Aurelius Antoninus, born in AD 121. Marcus Aurelius was an active devotee of the Stoic school of philosophy, another of whose doctrines was the universal brotherhood and equality of man. When the time came, he insisted that equal imperial rights should be vested in his rival candidate, which were duly but largely nominally exercised by Verus until his death. Of Antoninus and Marcus Aurelius, Gibbon wrote: 'Their united reigns are possibly the only period in history in which the happiness of a great people was the sole object of government' (*The History of the Decline and Fall of the Roman Empire*, I, 3). The volume in which those words first appeared was published in 1776; they still bear thinking about. By 'great people' Gibbon meant the Roman empire or commonwealth, and this was the period in which the way was being prepared for full rights for all citizens within it. Municipal governments were operating in the provinces, and where they proved moderately effective and acted within the laws and customs of Rome, they were allowed to work without much hindrance. Over a third of the senate itself came from the provinces, albeit chosen by the emperor, not the electorate.

It was perhaps because Hadrian left the administration in such good order that the twenty-three years of the reign of Antoninus, who died in AD 161, are remarkable for lack of incident. With the reports available to him of Hadrian's globe-trotting missions, he was able to spend most of his time at the centre of government in Rome. He did, however, make two adjustments to the frontiers of the empire. The eastern boundary of Upper Germany was advanced and strengthened; in Britain, a fortified turf wall, 60 km long, was built right across the country from the river Clyde to the Forth, some way north of Hadrian's Wall. Though the Antonine Wall, built by the Second, Sixth, and Twentieth legions, appears to have been abandoned, and perhaps dismantled, in about AD 165, Hadrian's Wall stood firm until about AD 400, when the Romans withdrew from Britain.

In his lifetime Antoninus fully justified the honorific surname of Pius, bestowed on him by the senate: his death, unlike that of most other emperors of Rome, was appropriately calm and dignified.

Though he died in his seventy-fifth year, his loss was treated as though he were still a young man. His death was said to have happened like this: having eaten rather too much

Alpine cheese at dinner, he was sick in the night, and had a fever the next day. The morning after that, recognizing that he was getting worse, in the presence of the prefects he entrusted the state and responsibility for his daughter to Marcus [Aurelius], and gave instructions that the gold statue of Fortune which traditionally stood in the emperor's bedroom should be handed over to him. Then he gave the password of 'equanimity' to the officer of the watch, turned over as if going to sleep, and died. . . . The senate deified him; everyone vied with everyone else in singing his praises. All, however, were agreed on his dedication, humanity, intellect, and goodness.
(*Scriptores Historiae Augustae*, Julius Capitolinus, *Antoninus Pius*, XII, XIII)

By contrast, the 'philosopher emperor' Marcus Aurelius had to spend most of his time in the field at the head of his armies, one of which brought back from an eastern campaign the most virulent plague of the Roman era, which spread throughout the whole empire. A confused picture emerges of his wars against the Parthians and against two dangerous Germanic tribes, the Marcomanni and Quadi, who at one point broke through the Danube frontier defences and penetrated as far as Aquileia at the head of the Adriatic Sea, before deciding not to chance their arm any further. Marcus Aurelius left to posterity the triumphal column in Rome which bears his name and records his victories over the Marcomanni (an inferior version of that of Trajan), and, rather unusually, a book of meditations, written in Greek. At his death in AD 180 at the age of 59, the empire was once again undergoing a period of general unease. As soon as one revolt was crushed or a barbarian invasion averted, another would break out, or threaten, in a different part of the empire.

GRADUAL DISINTEGRATION AD 180–284

The previous eighty-four years had seen just five emperors: during the next 104, there were no less than twenty-nine. What really started the rot was that alone of the five 'good' emperors, Marcus Aurelius had a son whom, with an upsurge of family feeling which belied his reputation as a philosopher, he had nominated as his successor. Marcus Aurelius had been 40

Figure 38 Detail from a triumphal arch: a gentle-looking, almost modest, Marcus Aurelius rides in a four-horse chariot in AD 176. This celebration of his victory over the Marcomanni had been delayed while he put down an insurrection in the east. Winged victory hovers above him. A trumpeter blows a *tuba*, the long horn used by the military to sound the advance and retreat. If the head and shoulders in the centre of the picture are those of Faustina, she was his late wife. Though various amours and other disloyal acts have been attributed to her, she was deified on her death in AD 175 and features frequently on coins. (*C. M. Dixon*)

when he assumed the imperial purple gown of an office for which he had been groomed for more than twenty years. Lucius Aurelius Commodus (AD 161–92) had a number of elder brothers who had died early: he was only 19 when he became emperor, and he proved to be a latter-day Nero. Like Nero, he showed initially some grasp of foreign and trade affairs; like Nero, he got himself into the hands of favourites and corruptible freedmen; like Nero, his private life was a disgrace and his public extravagances prodigious; like Nero, he fancied himself in the circus; and like Nero, he died ignominiously – a professional athlete was suborned to strangle him in his bath.

Whatever the nature of the conspiracy, it brought to office in his place a better man, Publius Helvius Pertinax, prefect of Rome and a former governor of Britain; but only temporarily, as an ominous pattern of events unfolded such as had followed the death of Nero. Pertinax, a disciplinarian, was murdered three months later by the imperial guard, who then offered the empire for sale to the highest bidder in terms of imperial hand-outs. The winner of this bizarre auction was Didius Salvius Julianus, an elderly senator, but there were out in the field three other serious contenders, each an army commander with several legions behind him. Lucius Septimius Severus (AD 146–211) in Pannonia was nearest to Rome, which he captured on 2 June AD 193 without a fight. Didius Julianus was stripped of office and put to death on the orders of the senate. Having disbanded the imperial guard and replaced it with men from his own legions, Severus set about coming to terms with his two rivals, Pescennius Niger in Syria and Clodius Albinus in Britain. This he finally did in a most conclusive fashion by defeating them in turn: Niger at Issus in AD 194, and Albinus at Lugdunum in Gaul in AD 197.

Severus was born in Leptis Magna in Africa. A professional soldier, he favoured those with the greater military experience when making civil appointments. He campaigned energetically to maintain the empire's frontiers in the east in the face of the marauding Parthians, and spent the last two and a half years of his life in Britain fending off the menaces of the northern tribes. It was probably in his time that the prefect of Rome, whose function was primarily military, was invested also with the main jurisdiction in matters of criminal law in and within 100 miles of the city, and the commander of the imperial guard, a military office, with similar jurisdiction over the rest of Italy and the

Figure 39   The Roman tradition that women took no part in public life
was broken by the wife of Septimius Severus, Julia Domna, who came
from a royal priestly family in Syria. According to Dio Cassius
(LXXXVIII. 18), when Caracalla succeeded his father, she dealt with
petitions and with his correspondence (in both Latin and Greek), and
held soirées and receptions for philosophers and scientists. She had an
equally formidable sister, Julia Maesa, who was the grandmother of
Elagabalus: Maesa's daughter was Julia Mammaea, who ran the empire
with her son, Alexander Severus. (*Antikensammlungen, Munich*)

provinces. After the fall and execution in AD 205 of Fulvius
Plautianus, who had performed the latter duty with rather too
much authority, Severus appointed in his place a noted legal
expert, Aemilius Papinianus (d. AD 212). Within the army itself,
the top jobs went to those with the best qualifications, not
necessarily those of the highest social rank. Severus improved
the lot of the legionaries by increasing their basic rate of pay to
match inflation (it had been static for a hundred years), and by
recognizing permanent liaisons as legal marriages – up until
then a legionary was not allowed to marry. It was probably
Severus, too, who improved the status of the ordinary soldier

by extending the civil practice to allow veterans to style themselves *honestiores* (men of privilege) as opposed to *humiliores* (men of
humble rank). As the distinction between citizens and non-
citizens became eroded, so this new form of class-discrimination
developed, which included separate punishments for the same
crime. Whereas *humiliores* could be sentenced to hard labour in
the mines, *honestiores* were merely banished for a short term. The
most common form of punishment for a minor offence was
flogging, from which *honestiores* were immune. Severus's philosophy of rule, which, according to Dio Cassius (**LXXVI.** 15), he
impressed upon his sons shortly before his death in AD 211, was
to pay the army well and to take no notice of anyone else. By
'anyone else' he meant, of course, the senate.

Severus had two unruly sons, Caracalla (AD 188–217) and
Geta (AD 189–212), whom he had nominated to rule jointly
after him. Caracalla (a nickname – it means a Gaulish great-
coat) resolved that aspect of the arrangement by murdering his
brother, and kept faith with his father's advice by increasing the
pay of the army by 50 per cent, thus initiating a financial crisis.
Some sources suggest that it was to get more taxes to repair this
crisis that he granted full citizenship to all free men in the
Roman empire. Whether or not that is so, it is to him in AD
212 that is attributed this final step in the process of universal
enfranchisement which had begun in the third century BC. While
attempting to extend the eastern front he was murdered in
Mesopotamia in AD 217, by a band of discontented officers
who preferred their own candidate, Macrinus, commander of
the imperial guard since Caracalla had done away with
Papinianus:

> There are many who say that Caracalla, after having had his
> brother killed, ordered Papinianus to play down the crime
> on his behalf in the senate and in public. Papinianus replied
> that it was easier to commit fratricide than to make excuses
> for it.
>
> (*Scriptores Historiae Augustae*, Aelius Spartianus, *Caracalla*, VIII)

Macrinus, though accepted by the senate, never actually got to
Rome. He continued the eastern war, only to be defeated and
killed the following year by detachments of his own troops in
Syria, who supported a 14-year-old supposed son, but actually a
distant cousin, of Caracalla. This was the notoriously depraved

and arrogant Elagabalus (AD 204–22), who lasted less than four years before being lynched by his own guards, having nominated as his successor his young first cousin, Alexander Severus (AD 205–35). That a 16-year-old could take office as emperor and rule for thirteen years with more than moderate success was due partly to the fact that he was a sensible, likeable lad who knew his limitations and was prepared to take advice, and partly to his mother, Julia Mammaea, who recognized who would give the soundest advice. His reign thus qualifies as the only imperial matriarchy in the history of the Roman empire. Indeed Alexander took his mother with him on campaign in Germany in AD 234, where the next year they were both set upon and murdered by mutinous soldiers at the fortress town of Mainz.

This was certainly the work of Maximinus (AD 173–238), a giant of a Thracian peasant who had risen through the ranks to become commander of the imperial guard. He now nominated himself as emperor, doubled the pay of the army, and continued the German campaign at its head. In AD 238 no fewer than five emperors died by various means and hands. The senate tired of Maximinus and put up its own candidate, Gordian, the 80-year-old governor of Africa, who extended the invitation to include also his son, Gordian II. They had hardly had time to pack their bags before the governor of Numidia, who was a supporter of Maximinus, attacked and defeated their soldiers. Gordian II was killed in the battle; his father committed suicide. Shortly afterwards, Maximinus invaded Italy, but was murdered by members of his own army. The senate had in the meantime replaced the Gordians with two further candidates of its own, who were in turn killed by the imperial guard in favour of Gordian III, son of Gordian II. Though he was only 13, this Gordian, with the help of a capable regent, enjoyed civil and military success until the regent died of an illness, and he himself was murdered in Mesopotamia in AD 244 while innocently collecting wild animals to take part in his triumphal procession in Rome for his victories in Persia.

While the next fourteen emperors came and violently went, the hostile peoples outside the frontiers gathered themselves for the kill. In Germany, the Goths, the Franks, and the Alamanni established the permanent threat to the Roman empire which ultimately led to its annihilation. In AD 259 the Parthians even managed to capture the emperor, Valerian, who spent the rest of his life uncomfortably in their hands. His son Gallienus, who had been joint ruler, carried on alone until in AD 268 he too fell to the more usual method, murder by his staff.

The threat of the empire being overrun from several directions at once was temporarily averted by Aurelian (AD 214–75), who became emperor in AD 270. In addition to evacuating the Roman garrisons in Dacia, he defeated the Alamanni, who on this, their fourth invasion of Italy, had got as far as Ariminum. He also dealt with two dangerous outbreaks of separatism. At the time of Gallienus, numerous petty emperors had surfaced in various parts of the empire. Some were readily disposed of; others were simply murdered by their own troops. In Gaul, however, Gaius Latinius Postumus had established an independent state, with its own senate. In AD 268 the local soldiery murdered Postumus, and then his three successors. The senate of Gaul now appointed Gaius Pius Tetricus as ruler, in which capacity he remained for three years until he surrendered to Aurelian's army. The *imperium Galliarum* was at an end, but in the meantime the influential city of Palmyra, under its formidable queen, Zenobia, was threatening Roman rule throughout the east. Attacks into Egypt and Asia Minor as far as the Bosporus were repelled, and Aurelian, after negotiating 100 miles of desert with his troops, destroyed Palmyra itself. Zenobia was brought back to Rome to walk, with Tetricus, in Aurelian's triumph; both were allowed to live, Zenobia with a generous pension, and Tetricus with a responsible job in local government in Italy. It was also Aurelian who built the great defensive wall round Rome itself. Murdered by his own staff, he earned the epitaph, 'He was loved by the people of Rome, and feared by the senate' (*Scriptores Historiae Augustae,* Flavius Vopiscus, *Aurelian,* L). The dreadful game of musical thrones continued after him, until AD 284, when yet another commander of the imperial guard, Valerius Diocletianus (AD 245–313), a Dalmatian of obscure and humble origin, emerged from the crush of contenders to be proclaimed by the troops.

PARTIAL RECOVERY: DIOCLETIAN AND CONSTANTINE AD 284–337

One aspect of the problem was not so much that the empire was falling apart, but that it had always consisted of two parts. Much of the region which comprised Macedonia and Cyrenaica and the lands to the east was Greek, or had been Hellenized before being occupied by Rome. The western part of the empire had received from Rome its first taste of a common culture and language overlaid on a society which was largely Celtic in origin. Diocletian was an organizer. In AD 286 he split the empire into east and west, and appointed a Dalmatian colleague, Maximian (d. AD 305), to rule the west and Africa. A further division of responsibilities followed in AD 292. Diocletian and Maximian remained senior emperors, with the title of Augustus, but Galerius, Diocletian's son-in-law, and Constantius (surnamed Chlorus, 'The Pale') were made deputy emperors with the title of Caesar. Galerius was given authority over the Danube provinces and Dalmatia, while Constantius took over Britain, Gaul, and Spain. Significantly, Diocletian retained all his eastern provinces and set up his regional headquarters at Nicomedia in Bithynia, where he held court with all the outward show of an eastern potentate, complete with regal trappings and elaborate ceremonial. The establishment of an imperial executive team had less to do with delegation than with the need to exercise

Figure 40 Caracalla introduced the *antoninianus*, a silver coin worth two *denarii*, which gradually became debased. By *c.* AD 293–6, the date of this particular coin, the metal was simply an alloy; it was minted in Britain by Allectus, who murdered Carausius in AD 293 and usurped his unconstitutional role. The figure and the letters round the rim stand, inappropriately, for peace – the ten-year-old rebellion was put down by Constantius in AD 296. The letters ML stand for *Moneta Londiniensis* (London Mint); established by Carausius, it was retained as an official source of issue until about AD 326. (×2)

closer supervision over all parts of the empire, and thus to lessen the chances of rebellion. There had already been trouble in the north, where in AD 286 the commander of the combined naval and military forces based at Boulogne, Aurelius Carausius, to avoid execution for embezzling stolen property, proclaimed himself emperor of Britain and even issued his own coins. This outbreak of *lèse-majesté* was not finally obliterated until AD 296.

Diocletian ruled for twenty-one years until, on 1 May AD 305, he took the unprecedented step of announcing from Nicomedia that he had abdicated, and offered Maximian no choice but to do the same. While his reign had been outwardly peaceful, the years of turmoil had left their mark on the administration of the empire and on its financial situation. Diocletian reorganized the provinces and Italy into 116 divisions, each governed by a *rector* or *praeses*, which were then grouped into twelve *dioceses* under a *vicarius* responsible to the appropriate emperor. He strengthened the army (while at the same time purging it of Christians), and introduced new policies for the supply of arms and provisions.

Diocletian's monetary reforms were equally wide-ranging, but though the new tax system he introduced was workable, if not always equitable, his bill in AD 301 to curb inflation by establishing maximum prices, wages, and freight charges fell into disuse, its effect having been that goods simply disappeared from the market. Its interest today lies in its comparisons, even though or because these are much as one would expect. Ordinary wine was twice the price of beer, while named vintages were almost four times as much as *vin ordinaire*. Pork mince cost half as much again as beef mince, and about the same as prime sea fish. River fish were cheaper. A pint of fresh quality olive oil was more expensive than the same amount of vintage wine; there was a cheaper oil as well. Fattened goose was prohibitive; ten dormice cost about as much as one chicken. A carpenter could expect twice the wages of a farm labourer or a sewer cleaner, all with meals included. A teacher of shorthand or arithmetic might earn half as much again per pupil as a primary-school teacher; grammar-school teachers earned four times as much as primary-school teachers, and teachers of rhetoric five times as much. Baths' attendants, those who guarded the clothes of bathers, and barbers were all paid the same rate per customer.

Somehow assured or confident of his own safety, Diocletian had built for his retirement a palace near Salona, on the coast of his native Dalmatia, round the ruins of which the modern town of Split stands. Here he lived until his death in AD 313, doing nothing more active than gardening and studying philosophy, and refusing to take sides when the system of government he had devised almost immediately foundered. When he retired, Diocletian had promoted Galerius and Constantius to the posts of Augustus, and appointed two new Caesars. The troubles broke out when Constantius died at York in AD 306, and his troops proclaimed his son Constantine as their leader. Encouraged by this development, Maxentius, son of Maximian, had himself set up as emperor and took control of Italy and Africa, whereupon his father came out of his involuntary retirement and insisted on having back his former imperial command. The situation degenerated into chaos. At one point in AD 308 there seem to have been six men styling themselves Augustus, whereas Diocletian's system allowed for only two. Galerius died in AD 311, having on his deathbed revoked Diocletian's anti-Christian edicts. Matters were not fully resolved until AD 324, when Constantine defeated and executed his last surviving rival. The empire once again had a single ruler, and against all the odds he lasted some years yet.

Constantine was born in Naissus in Upper Moesia in about AD 290, his father subsequently being forced to divorce his mother (a former barmaid) and marry Maximian's daughter. His appellation 'the Great' is justified on two counts. Under Diocletian especially, the Christians had had a terrible time. In AD 313, while the struggle for imperial power was at its height, Constantine initiated the Edict of Milan – Milan, not Rome, was now the administrative centre of the government of Italy – which gave Christians (and others) freedom of worship and exemption from any religious ceremonial. It is said that before the battle of the Milvian Bridge in AD 312, at which he enticed Maxentius to abandon his safe position behind the Aurelian Wall and then drove most of his army into the Tiber, Constantine had dreamed of the sign of Christ. Thereafter, though he was not actually baptized until just before his death in AD 337, he regarded himself as a man of the god of the Christians, and can therefore claim to be the first Christian emperor or king. In AD 325 he assembled at Nicaea in Bithynia 318 bishops, each elected by his community, to debate and affirm some principles of their faith. The result, known as the Nicene Creed, is now part of the Roman Catholic mass and the Anglican service of communion. And, in AD 330, he established the seat of government of the Roman empire at Byzantium (which he renamed Constantinople, 'City of Constantine'), thus ensuring that a Roman (but Hellenized and predominantly Christian) empire would survive the inevitable loss of its western part. Its capital stood, until the middle of the fifteenth century, as a barrier between the forces of the east and the as yet ill-organized tribes and peoples of Europe, each struggling to find a permanent identity and culture.

To the Jews Constantine was ambivalent: while the Edict of Milan is also known as the Edict of Toleration, Judaism was seen as a rival to Christianity, and among other measures he forbade the conversion of pagans to its practices. In time he became even more uncompromising towards the pagans themselves, enacting a law against divination and finally banning sacrifices. He also destroyed temples and confiscated temple lands and treasures, which gave him much-needed funds to fuel his personal extravagances. His reign constituted, however, a series of field days for architects, whom he encouraged to celebrate the religious revolution by reinventing the basilica as a dramatic ecclesiastical edifice. A general of considerable dynamism, he developed Diocletian's reforms, and completed the division of the military into two arms: frontier forces, and permanent reserves, who could be sent anywhere at short notice. He changed the system of command so that normally the posts of civil governor and military commander were separate. He disbanded the imperial guard, and established a chief of staff to assume control of all military operations and army discipline; the praetorian prefects (commanders of the imperial guard), who had hitherto held military ranks while also being involved in civil affairs, under him became supreme appeal judges and chief ministers of finance.

THE FALL OF ROME

Constantine had intended that on his death the rule of the empire should devolve to a team of four: his three sons, Constantius (d. AD 361), Constans (d. AD 350), and Constantine II (d. AD 340), and his nephew Dalmatius. To form a tetrarchy on a dynastic principle was, however, more than the system could stand. Dalmatius was murdered, the brothers bickered, their armies fought, and the empire was in splinters once again.

The pieces were retrieved after Valentinian (AD 321–75) was nominated as emperor by the troops at Nicaea, on condition that he appoint a joint ruler.

> Now, after Valentinian had been acclaimed emperor in Bithynia, he gave orders that the army should march in two days' time, and called a meeting of his senior officers, as though he intended to seek sound advice rather than follow his own inclinations. When he enquired who would be the best person to be his partner in running the empire, everyone was silent, except Dagalaifus, the master of the cavalry, who answered confidently: 'If you love your family, great emperor, you have a brother; if you love the state, choose someone else to invest with this office.'
>
> Valentinian was not pleased, but made no comment, hiding his thoughts. By a forced march, the army reached Nicomedia on 1 March [AD 364], where he appointed his brother Valens as chief of his personal staff, with the rank of tribune. Then, after arriving at Constantinople, he gave considerable thought to the matter. Having concluded that he was already overwhelmed by the amount of urgent business and that there should be no further delay, on 28 March he publicly presented Valens on the outskirts of the city and proclaimed him Augustus. There was universal acceptance of the appointment – no one dared oppose it.
>
> (Ammianus Marcellinus, *History*, XXVI, 4)

Valentinian and Valens (*c.* AD 328–78) made an amicable east-west division. The empire was briefly united again in AD 394 under Theodosius (*c.* AD 346–95). It was he who established Christianity as the official religion of the empire. It was also he who revenged the lynching of one of his army commanders by inviting the citizens of Thessalonica to a show at the circus and then massacring them in their seats, a lapse for which the Archbishop of Milan persuaded him to do public penance. Under his sons, Arcadius (*c.* AD 378–408) and Honorius (AD 385–423), the eastern and western parts of the Roman empire finally each went their own way.

At some point in the fourth century AD a fierce nomadic people known as the Huns set out inexorably westwards from their homelands on the plains of central Russia, triggering off similar and equally destructive movements on the part of the tribes in their way. They displaced the Alani who lived mainly between the rivers Dnieper and Dniester, and who then displaced the Vandals from their territories between the Vistula and the Rhine, who in turn swept right through Gaul and Spain, and down into North Africa. Also displaced in the orgy of migration were the Goths, who bordered on the Roman empire immediately on the other side of the lower Danube and who had fought implacably with Rome before. Britain was now abandoned to the determined waves of Picts, Scots, and Saxons who had threatened to overwhelm the land, and its legions were rushed to the final defence, no longer of the empire, but of Rome itself.

In AD 410 Rome was captured and sacked by Alaric the Goth (d. AD 411), after he had only the previous year accepted a bribe to go away. Though Pope Leo (d. AD 461) managed in AD 452 to negotiate terms with Attila the Hun (*c.* AD 406–53) to leave Italy after he had ravaged much of it, in AD 455 it was the turn of the Vandals: Rome was sacked once more, this time from the sea. Finally, in AD 476, Odoacer (d. AD 493), a German mercenary captain, deposed the emperor Romulus Augustulus and informed Zeno (d. AD 491), emperor of the eastern Roman empire, that he would be happy to rule as king of Italy under Zeno's jurisdiction. Effectively, the Roman empire in the west was at an end. The Roman Catholic Church now assumed the role of unifying the lands and peoples which had formerly been Roman, organizing its sphere of influence along Roman lines.

For truly catastrophic disasters, there is rarely a single cause. Civilizations less stable or well-organized than Rome have survived economic failure, political and administrative incompetence, plague, class divisions, corruption in high places, decline of moral standards, and the necessity of radically changing the structure and status of the work force. Ultimately, what hastened the end was the failure of the very instrument by which the empire had been founded, the Roman army. The policy of dividing it into frontier forces and mobile field forces which could be dispatched to trouble spots had its disadvantages. However effective communications might be, the infantry had to march to its destination – in training, recruits were required to march 32 km in five hours, but that would be about the most that an army could travel on foot in a day. The creation of more mobile armies simply meant that each one was weaker, at a time when heavy losses had been incurred in the civil wars in which prospective emperors engaged and in fighting off the invasions of Italy and of Gaul.

The eastern Roman empire, largely by reason of its geographical situation, was bypassed by the ant-like hordes of invaders. Its capital, Byzantium, had first been reconstructed in the time of Septimius Severus not just as a Roman city, but modelled on Rome itself, on and around seven hills. The building of a racecourse on the lines of the Circus Maximus where there was insufficient space for it, was not beyond the skill and ingenuity of the architects. It was constructed on the flattened summit of a hill, with one end of the stadium suspended over the edge on massive vaulted supports. Eastern influence led to the development of a distinctive style of Byzantine architecture, with the dome the predominant feature, and interiors richly decorated. In AD 532, during the reign of Justinian, much of the city was destroyed during what is known as the Nika rebellion, which began as a riot between two sets of fans, the Blues and Greens, in the stadium, and developed into a full-scale revolt against his authority. The revolt was, with difficulty, quelled, but the damage caused enabled him to exploit his own hobby of building, at a time when the golden age of Byzantine architecture had just been reached. Among four major new churches was the sensational St Sophia, designed by Anthemius, the main dome of which was built, unusually, on a square base and was replaced in AD 555 by one with forty arched windows around its circumference. St Sophia survives, but since 1453 has been a mosque.

Justinian ruled from AD 527 to 565, and is said to have been 83 when he died. He was born in Illyricum, the son of a Slavonic peasant, and was appointed joint emperor in AD 527 by his uncle Justin, who died a few months later, having risen through the ranks of the army to be emperor, still, it was alleged, unable to read or write. He had not, however, spared the education of his nephew, whose ambitious aims included stamping out corruption in government, refining and upholding the law, uniting the churches in the east, and taking Christianity forcibly to the barbarians in the west, thus recovering for the empire the territories that it had lost. In pursuit of this last aim, his skilled generals Narses, formerly employed as an imperial eunuch, and Belisarius tore into the barbarian kingdoms and restored to the empire, though only temporarily, its former African provinces and northern Italy, including the city of Rome itself. At the same time Justinian himself recaptured southern Spain while that region was in the throes of a civil war.

Before becoming emperor, Justinian had committed the solecism of marrying an actress called Theodora. Until her death in AD 548, however, she proved an admirable foil and a supportive wife, on the one hand standing up for persecuted members of the heretical Monophysite sect whose views she supported, and on the other comforting and encouraging her husband at times of stress, notably during the Nika rebellion. While the eastern empire was largely Greek in its *mores*, it still upheld Roman law. The Justinian Code (AD 529) brought together all valid imperial laws. In addition he issued a revised and up-to-date edition (AD 534) of the works of the classical jurists, and a textbook on Roman law (AD 533). He is also credited with introducing into Europe the culture of the silk-worm.

After Justinian, the eastern empire was Roman only in name. In 1053 the Church of the east split with the Church of Rome and in due course begat the Church of Russia. On 29 May 1453, Constantinople and its emperor Constantine XI fell to the Turks and the forces of Islam, who had already overrun what remained of the empire's narrow footholds along the coast of the Sea of Marmara.

THE LEGACY OF ROME

The remarkable thing about the Roman civilization is not that it ultimately collapsed, but that from such minute beginnings it survived for so long under so many external and internal pressures. It lasted long enough and the pressures were resisted firmly enough for so many of what were Roman practices, even before the Christian era, to become entrenched in modern life.

Except for the addition of three letters, the alphabet used today for the English language, as well as for the Romance languages (French, Italian, Spanish, Portuguese, and Romanian), German, Scandinavian, and other European languages, is that which the Romans developed and refined for their own language. Further, the Romance languages themselves are firmly based on Latin, as is one-third of the English language. The

Figure 41 The inscription on this first-century or early second-century
AD sepulchral chest in the form of a house reads: 'Marcus Junius
Hamillus, freedman of Marcus, for himself and his dearest wife, Junia
Pieris'. The carved lettering is of an informal kind, reflecting the style of
advertisements or public announcements painted on walls with a brush.
The basic Latin alphabet consisted of twenty-one characters: Y and Z
were added in later times for the spelling of words borrowed from the
Greek. J, U, and W were introduced in the Middle Ages. (*British Museum*)

success of Latin as the foundation of so much of modern
language is not just due to the fact that it was possible to use
it eloquently for the expression of literary forms – and without a
close acquaintance with Latin literature on the part of writers in
other languages, there would be virtually no English or
European literature before about 1800 – but that it could be
employed so precisely to express points of law, science, theology,
philosophy, architecture, agriculture, and medicine. As such it

was the language of scholarship, and prose, in western Europe during the Middle Ages and the Renaissance; it is the language of the Roman Catholic Church; and it survives intact within the English language in the form of many tags and phrases. While it was not in the Romans' nature, or necessarily in their interest, to invent startling labour-saving devices, their systematic attitude to measurement enabled them to establish the basis of a calendar which has never been improved upon, and to devise methods to assess distances with great accuracy. They turned building into a science and gave a new impetus to the science of hydraulics. The contribution of Roman law to European law is incalculable, and from the Romans come the traditions of impartial justice and trial by jury. Banking, public hospitals, the postal system, the daily newspaper, the fire service, central heating, glass windows, blocks of flats, sanitation, drainage and sewers, social benefits, and public education are all Roman institutions. So is that universal common bond and basis of social life throughout the modern world, which they called *familia* (the household) and we recognize as the family, or the family unit.

Appendix 1

THE ROMAN CALENDAR

The reformed calendar which Julius Caesar instituted in 46 BC, on the advice of the Peripatetic Alexandrian philosopher and astronomer Sosigenes, enabled the traditional agricultural year, based on the circuit of the earth round the sun, to be reconciled with the duration of a complete revolution of the moon round the earth. His year of 365 days (366 every fourth year) consisted of 7 months of 31 days, 4 of 30 days, and 1 of 28 days (29 every fourth year). A slight, and temporary, adjustment had to be made in the time of Augustus when it was discovered that the *pontifices* had misinterpreted the instructions and had decreed a leap year every three years instead of four. The year was still actually 11 minutes 14 seconds too long, which it remained until Pope Gregory XIII in the sixteenth century corrected the error and adjusted the incidence of the leap year so that it does not fall on the opening year of a new century unless that year is divisible by 400. Thus the year 2000 will be a leap year; 2100 will not.

Each month was divided into three parts by three special days: *kalendae* (the calends) always fell on the first day of the month; *idus* (the ides) signified the notional day of the full moon, and was the 15th day of March, May, July, and October – the months of 31 days – and the 13th of all the rest; *nonae* (the nones) occurred on the 9th day before the ides in each case, including in the calculation the day at each end of the period. Thus the nones of March was 7 March, that is the 9th day before the ides. A date was always reckoned according to the number of days it fell before the next special day, both that day and the special day being included in the calculation. Thus 16 March was known as the 'the 17th day before the calends of April'.

Certain days were given over to religious and other festivals and celebrations, almost all of which took place on dates of an uneven number, which were regarded as being lucky. Other days were designated *fasti*, indicating that civil and judicial business could be conducted; *comitiales*, on which a meeting of an assembly could be held; and *nefasti*, on which neither could take place. The Romans worked an eight-day week, the eighth day by our reckoning, the ninth by theirs, being known as *nundinae*; it was the day on which traditionally the farmers downed tools and went to market.

The Roman day was divided into twelve hours of equal length, from sunrise to sunset, and likewise during the night. Thus the length of an hour, and the hour itself, varied according to the season of the year. The ninth hour of the day gave its name to Nones, a church service held at about 1500 hours; at some point in the Middle Ages this was brought forward to the sixth hour, that is about 1200. The name Nones persisted, however, and gave the word 'noon' its meaning of the middle of the day. So when we speak of a.m., we mean *ante meridiem* (before the middle of the day); p.m. is *post meridiem* (after the middle of the day). Sundials or water-clocks, or a combination of both, were employed to tell the hour.

Appendix 2

ROMAN NUMERALS

The basic symbols by which all Roman numerals were and still are expressed are:

I = 1   (a single digit)
V = 5   (a graphic representing five fingers)
X = 10   (the fingers of two hands joined)
L = 50   (adapted from a Chalcidic sign)
C = 100   (adapted from a Chalcidic sign; it is also the first letter of the word for a hundred, *centum*)
D = 500   (half the Chalcidic sign Ⓓ, which represented a thousand)
M = 1,000 (the first letter of the word for a thousand, *mille*: not used separately as a numeral before the second century AD)

Numbers other than these were expressed by adding symbols after the higher numeral, e.g. VI = 6, XII = 12, CLXI = 161; or by subtracting those that preceded the higher numeral, e.g. IV = 4, XL = 40; or by a combination of both processes, e.g. XLI = 41, CDXIII = 413. In medieval times and beyond, dates were represented by Roman numerals, e.g. MCCCLXII = 1362. The year 1996 would be MCMXCVI.

Towards the end of the republic, thousands were denoted by a line above the numeral, e.g. $\overline{V}$ = 5,000, $\overline{IX}$ = 9,000. Hundreds of thousands were denoted by additional lines on each side, e.g. $|\overline{V}|$ = 500,000, $|\overline{X}|$ = 1,000,000.

Calculating was done with the help of an abacus, or by a complex counting system involving the use of the fingers, finger-joints, and thumbs of both hands.

Appendix 3

DATES IN THE HISTORY OF ROME

BC

c. 1220	Sack of Troy
c. 1000	Latins settle in Latium
753	Traditional date of founding of Rome
c. 625	Historical founding of Rome
510	Ejection of last king of Rome
509	Establishment of republic
505	Defeat of Etruscans at Aricia
496	Romans defeat Latins at Lake Regillus
c. 494	Office of tribune of the people instituted
450	Publication of the Twelve Tables
444	Office of censor instituted
390	Gauls sack Rome, but withdraw in return for ransom
367	First plebeian consul elected
356	Rutilus first plebeian dictator
338	Latin league of states dissolved
327–290	Samnite wars
321	Disaster at Caudine Forks
283	Final capitulation of Etruscans
275	Defeat of Pyrrhus of Epirus
264–241	First Punic War
241	Sicily becomes first Roman province
218–202	Second Punic War
218	Hannibal invades Italy
217	Roman defeat at Lake Trasimene
216	Roman defeat at Cannae
202	Hannibal defeated at Zama

200–167	Wars against Macedonia
184	Cato elected censor
	Death of the playwright Plautus
169	Death of Ennius, father of Latin poetry
153	Year begins on 1 January
149–146	Third Punic War
146	Destruction of Carthage
133	Tiberius Gracchus tribune of the people
	Pergamum bequeathed to Rome (becomes the province of Asia)
123	Gaius Gracchus tribune of the people
107	First consulship of Marius
104–101	Slave revolt in Sicily
91–89	Social War
88–63	Wars against Mithridates
82–80	Sulla dictator
74	Bithynia and Cyrenaica become provinces of Rome
73–71	Slave revolt of Spartacus
67	Pompey defeats the pirates
63	Consulship of Cicero. Catiline conspiracy
	Syria (including Judaea until 40 BC) becomes a province
59	First consulship of Caesar. Formation of triumvirate
58–50	Caesar's Gallic wars
c. 55	Death of the poet Lucretius
49	Caesar crosses the Rubicon
	Caesar's first dictatorship
48	Battle of Pharsalus
44	Assassination of Caesar
43	First consulship of Octavian. Formation of triumvirate for five years.
	Murder of Cicero
42	Battle of Philippi
31	Battle of Actium
	Egypt taken over by Rome
27	Octavian becomes *princeps* and assumes the name of Augustus
19	Death of Virgil
8	Death of the poet Horace

DATES IN THE HISTORY OF ROME

AD

9	Varian disaster
14	Death of Augustus
17	Death of the historian Livy
18	Death of the poet Ovid
c. 30	Crucifixion of Jesus
43	Invasion of Britain
61	Revolt of Boudicca in Britain
64	Great fire of Rome
66–73	First Jewish War
69	Year of four emperors
78–84	Agricola governor of Britain
79	Eruption of Vesuvius
80	Opening of Colosseum
101	Trajan invades Dacia
104	Death of the poet Martial
c. 117	Death of the historian Tacitus
117	Death of Trajan and accession of Hadrian
	Roman empire at its greatest extent
c. 122	Building of Pantheon
c. 127	Hadrian's Wall completed
131–5	Final revolt of the Jews
c. 140	Death of the poet Juvenal
167	Barbarian invasions across Danube
180	Death of Marcus Aurelius
212	Roman citizenship for all free inhabitants of the empire
251	Gothic invasions of the empire begin
286	Diocletian separates eastern and western empires
330	Constantine makes Byzantium capital of empire
410	Rome sacked by Alaric the Goth
455	Vandals sack Rome
476	End of Roman empire in the west
1453	Fall of Constantinople and end of Roman empire in the east

READING LIST

General

Boardman, John, Griffin, Jasper and Murray, Oswyn (eds), *The Oxford History of the Roman World*, Oxford University Press, Oxford and New York, 1991.

Cary, Max and Scullard, H. H., *History of Rome: down to the age of Constantine*, Macmillan, London, rev. edn 1980; St Martin's Press, New York, 3rd edn 1976.

Cornell, Tim and Matthews, John, *Atlas of the Roman World*, Facts on File, New York, new edn 1982.

Hammond, N. G. L. and Scullard, H. H. (eds), *The Oxford Classical Dictionary*, Oxford University Press, Oxford and New York, 2nd edn 1970.

Ireland, S. (ed.), *Roman Britain: a sourcebook*, Routledge, London and New York, 1991.

Keppie, Lawrence, *Scotland's Roman Remains: an introduction and handbook*, John Donald, Edinburgh, rev. edn 1990.

McEvedy, Colin, *The Penguin Atlas of Ancient History*, Penguin, London and New York, 1967.

Salway, Peter, *Roman Britain*, Oxford University Press, Oxford and New York, new edn 1984.

———— *The Oxford Illustrated History of Roman Britain*, Oxford University Press, Oxford and New York, 1993.

Tripp, Edward, *Collins Reference Dictionary of Classical Mythology*, Harper-Collins, Glasgow, new edn 1988; as *Meridian Handbook of Classical Mythology*, Dutton, New York, 1974.

Chapter 1

Holloway, R. Ross, *The Archaeology of Early Rome and Latium*, Routledge, London and New York, 1994.

Scullard, H. H., *A History of the Roman World 753 to 146 BC*, Routledge, London and New York, new edn 1991.

Chapter 2

Beard, Mary and Crawford, Michael, *Rome in the Late Republic: problems and interpretations*, Duckworth, London, 1985.

Crawford, Michael, *The Roman Republic*, Fontana, London, 2nd rev. edn 1992; Harvard University Press, Cambridge, Mass., 2nd edn 1993.

Hart, B. H. Liddell, *Scipio Africanus: greater than Napoleon*, Greenhill, London, new edn 1992; Presidio, California, new edn 1992.

Rawson, Elizabeth, *Cicero: a portrait*, Bristol Classical Press, Bristol, new edn 1983.

Chapter 3

Millar, Fergus, *The Emperor in the Roman World*, Duckworth, London, new edn 1984; Cornell University Press, Ithaca, new edn 1992.

Shotter, David, *Augustus Caesar*, Routledge, London and New York, 1991.

———— *Tiberius Caesar*, Routledge, London and New York, 1992.

Syme, Ronald, *The Roman Revolution*, Oxford University Press, Oxford and New York, new edn 1960.

Webster, Graham, *The Roman Invasion of Britain*, Batsford, London, new edn 1993.

Wells, Colin, *The Roman Empire*, Fontana, London, 2nd edn 1992.

Chapter 4

Cohn-Sherbok, Dan, *Atlas of Jewish History*, Routledge, London and New York, 1994.

Ferguson, John, *The Religions of the Roman Empire*, Thames and Hudson, London, 1970; Cornell University Press, Ithaca, 1970.

Green, Miranda J., *The Gods of Roman Britain*, Shire Publications, Aylesbury, 1983.

Ogilvie, R. M., *The Romans and Their Gods: in the age of Augustus*, Hogarth Press, London, new edn 1986.

Chapter 5

Auguet, Roland, *Cruelty and Civilization: the Roman games*, Routledge, London and New York, new edn 1994.

Carcopino, Jerome, *Daily Life in Ancient Rome*, Penguin, London and New York, new edn 1991.

Crook, J. A., *Law and Life of Rome*, Thames and Hudson, London, new edn 1984.

Gardner, Jane F., *Women in Roman Law and Society*, Routledge, London, new edn 1987.

———— and Wiedemann, Thomas, *The Roman Household: a sourcebook*, Routledge, London and New York, 1991.

Greene, Kevin, *The Archaeology of the Roman Economy*, Batsford, London, 1986; University of California Press, Berkeley, 1991.

The Roman Cookery of Apicius, tr. and adapted for the modern kitchen by John Edwards, Rider, London, 1984; Hunter & Marks, Washington, 1985.

Shelton, Jo-Ann, *As the Romans Did: a sourcebook in Roman social history*, Oxford University Press, New York and Oxford, 1988.

Chapter 6

Hamey, L. A. and J. A., *The Roman Engineers*, Cambridge University Press, Cambridge and New York, 1981.

Leacroft, Richard and Helen, *Theatre and Playhouse: an illustrated survey of theatre building from ancient Greece to the present day*, Methuen, London and New York, 1984.

Ling, Roger, *Roman Painting*, Cambridge University Press, Cambridge and New York, 1991.

Ramage, Nancy H. and Andrew, *The Cambridge Illustrated History of Roman Art*, Cambridge University Press, Cambridge and New York, 1991.

Strong, Donald E., *Roman Art*, Penguin, London and New York, 2nd rev. edn 1980.

Ward-Perkins, J. B., *Roman Imperial Architecture*, Penguin, London, 1981; Yale University Press, New Haven, 1981.

Chapter 7

Readable translations of the works of all the major authors mentioned in this book are available in Penguin Classics. Good modern versions in English of Apuleius, Catullus, Juvenal, Lucan, Ovid, and Propertius are published by Oxford University Press. Loeb Classical Library editions (Harvard University Press) include the Latin texts as well.

Grant, Michael (ed.), *Latin Literature: an anthology*, Penguin, London, and New York, new edn 1979.

Griffin, Jasper, *Virgil*, Oxford University Press, Oxford and New York, 1986.

Highet, Gilbert, *The Classical Tradition: Greek and Roman influences on western literature*, Oxford University Press, Oxford and New York, 1987.

Howatson, M. C. (ed.), *The Oxford Companion to Classical Literature*, Oxford University Press, Oxford and New York, 2nd edn 1989.

Lyne, R. O. A. M., *The Latin Love Poets from Catullus to Horace*, Oxford University Press, Oxford and New York, 1980.

Mellor, Ronald, *Tacitus*, Routledge, London and New York, 1994.

Sowerby, Robin (ed.), *Dryden's Aeneid: a selection with commentary*, Bristol Classical Press, Bristol, 1986.

Williams, Gordon, *The Nature of Roman Poetry*, Oxford University Press, Oxford and New York, new edn 1983.

Chapter 8

Campbell, Brian, *The Roman Army: a sourcebook*, Routledge, London and New York, 1994.

Hackett, General Sir John (ed.), *Warfare in the Ancient World*, Sidgwick & Jackson, London, 1989; Facts on File, New York, 1990.

Keppie, Lawrence, *The Making of the Roman Army: from republic to empire*, Batsford, London, 1984.

Webster, Graham, *The Roman Imperial Army*, Black, London, 3rd edn 1985.

Chapter 9

Grant, Michael, *The Climax of Rome: the final achievement of the ancient world*, Weidenfeld, new edn 1993.

Jenkyns, Richard (ed.), *The Legacy of Rome: a new appraisal*, Oxford University Press, Oxford and New York, 1992.

Jones, A. H. M., *The Decline of the Ancient World*, Longman, Harlow, new edn 1975.

INDEX

Note: All Latin words and phrases in the text are indexed. Names are listed in their most usually recognizable form. *Indicates a quotation. Italic figures refer to the caption to an illustration. Bold figures indicate a main item.

origin 18; Livy on repealing of
Oppian Law 109–10
Trier 138
triumph 14, 50, *60*, 61, 138, *139*,
141, 182, 185, *186*, 190, 191
Trojan War, Troy 4, 5, 107, 144,
146, 158, 205
tuba 186
Tulingi *176*
Tullus Hostilius 7
Turnus 5, 158
Tusculum 11, 12, 23
Twelve Tables **18–20**, 205
Tyre 126

Udall, Nicolas 151
Umbria 151, 159

Valens 196
Valentinian **196**; Ammianus on
196
Valerian 190–1
Vandals 197, 207
Varro 1*, 13*
Varus, Publius Quintilius 177,
207
Vedius Pollio: Pliny the Elder on
114
Venus 4, 80, 83, *137*, 152, *157*
Venusia 154
Vercingetorix 46
Verona 153
Verres 41
Vertumnus 83
Verus, Lucius 183, 184
Vespasian 67, **68–71**, 73, 96,
100, 104, 167, 169; Suetonius
on 68–9
Vesta 2, 83, 87, 92, 95
vestal virgins 2, 14, 84, 87, 92–3,
95, 108; Tacitus on selection of
93
vestibulum 133
Vesuvius, Mount 72, 99, 169,
170, 207; Pliny the Younger on

eruption of 72
Via Latina 35
vicarius 193
vigiles 173
villa rustica 133
villa urbana 133
Vinalia Rustica 91
Vindex, Gaius Julius 65
Vindolanda 121
Vipsania 52
Virgil 4–5*, 26*, 90*, 103, 146*,
148*, 149, 154, **156–9**, 206;
Tennyson on 147; T. S. Eliot on
159
Vistula, river 197
Vitellius 66, **67**, 167; Suetonius
on 67
Volturnus 83, 95
volumen 145
Vopiscus 191*
Vulcan 83, 95

Weser, river 177
Wight, Isle of 69
women, place of 3, 4, 13, 44, 68,
73, 87, 88, 94–5, 99, 105,
107–12, 116, 117, 120, 136,
153, 163, *182*, *186*, *188*, 190,
191, 199; Catullus on rights
108; Cicero on rights 107–8;
Livy on Cloelia 11-12, on
demonstrations against Oppian
Law 109–10; Martial on female
gladiators 110; Pliny the
Younger on death of young
bride 108, on dowry 108–9;
Sallust on Sempronia; Tacitus
on Pompeia Paulina 111–12

Zama, battle of 28, 205
Zela, battle of 47
Zeno *104*, 197
Zenobia 191
Zeus *161*